THE
UNRESPONSIVE
BYSTANDER: Why doesn't he help?

The Richard M. Elliott Memorial Award 1968

In memory of Richard M. Elliott (1887–1969) founder and editor for forty-five years of the Century Psychology Series.

Kenneth MacCorquodale
Gardner Lindzey
Kenneth E. Clark
EDITORS

1962 BERNARD RIMLAND: *Infantile autism: The syndrome and its implications for a neutral theory of behavior*

1963 EDWARD E. JONES: *Ingratiation: A social psychological analysis*

1964 JACK BLOCK: *The challenge of response sets: Unconfounding meaning, acquiescence, and social desirability in the MMPI*

1965 MERLE B. TURNER: *Philosophy and the science of behavior*

1966 ULRIC NEISSER: *Cognitive psychology*

1967 ELEANOR J. GIBSON: *Principles of perceptual learning and development*

THE
UNRESPONSIVE
BYSTANDER: Why doesn't he help?

BIBB LATANÉ
Ohio State University

JOHN M. DARLEY
Princeton University

PRENTICE-HALL, INC.
Englewood Cliffs, New Jersey

Printed in the United States of America

ISBN: 0-13-938613-0

Library of Congress Catalog Card Number: 79-123548

10 9 8 7 6 5

PRENTICE-HALL INTERNATIONAL, INC., *London*
PRENTICE-HALL OF AUSTRALIA, PTY. LTD., *Sydney*
PRENTICE-HALL OF CANADA, LTD., *Toronto*
PRENTICE-HALL OF INDIA PRIVATE LIMITED, *New Delhi*
PRENTICE-HALL OF JAPAN, INC., *Tokyo*

PREFACE

Over the past four years we have been engaged in a program of research into the determinants of bystander intervention in emergencies. After analyzing the motives and processes which underlie intervention, we have theorized about a variety of factors which might affect the intervention process. Hypotheses were developed from this theory and they have been tested in a variety of experimental situations, both in the laboratory and in the field. The results of these experiments have taught us a great deal about the intervention process. In general, they have provided good support for the hypotheses that stimulated them. They have also provided some surprises. This monograph presents the hypotheses, the confirmations, and the surprises.

Undergraduates and graduate students probably will enjoy making the discovery that the outcomes of research are not so inevitably predicted in advance as an uncritical reading of professional journals might lead them to believe, and they are one of the audiences for whom this book is intended. We also think that it will give our professional colleagues a more complete account of our research than has previously been available. Finally, we believe in the existence of that legendary totem figure of all academic authors, the intelligent, well-informed layman who wants to find out more about the world in which he lives.

So we hope that this book may have some interest for the general public as well as for our professional colleagues. This hope has led us to write in a style designed to appeal to both audiences—a risky ambition, for such attempts often end up appealing to neither. We apologize to any general readers for whatever jargon inevitably slipped through our defenses into print and for possible overdoses of percentages, significance levels, and other esoteric numbers which we felt were necessary for our fellow professionals. We apologize to our colleagues for occasionally explaining what will be obvious to them and for dwelling on what will be to them elementary points. To both groups we apologize for inelegancies, inconsistencies, and, above all, for an occasional, irresistible pun.

Many people helped us during the course of this research—indeed, without them it could not have been completed, and we would like to acknowledge our indebtedness and express our gratitude to them. Our first debt is to our wives, and in our case the debt goes beyond the usual allusions to superhuman domestic bliss and tranquillity, because both of them were considerably involved in the work. We are like most people about deadlines; without Jane's good humor and competence through long, late hours we would have missed rather more than we did. Susan with equal good humor and competence set up and ran several of the studies. Both of them deserve considerable credit for whatever success the research has achieved, and it is a great pleasure to acknowledge in public what, for reasons that any married man will understand, we have avoided admitting in private.

For the past several years, it is no secret that government support for scientific research has been both reduced in scope and uncertain in timing. In the face of this, the National Science Foundation has generously funded our research for the past four years and Carl Backman and Charles Wright have worked hard to create certainties and security for it when both have been hard to come by. We are grateful to the National Science Foundation and to them.

Many of our readers will be familiar with the division of labor that prevails in academic circles, while others will need to be told that, in order that the faculty may be free for dignified thought, much of the actual conduct of research devolves on graduate students. Whenever a student's contributions can be described and acknowledged, we have done so. Several students, however, were helpful at various stages of the research, have worked devotedly with us for several years, and have shared with us their insights about people's reactions to emergencies. Harvey Allen, Howard Cappell, Donald Elman, Keith Gerritz, Thomas Moriarity, Judith Rodin, and Lee Ross will all find their ideas in the following pages.

Many of our colleagues read, criticized, and greatly improved this manuscript. We suspect that our gratitude to them is exceeded only by our misunderstanding of their suggestions. Our thanks to Timothy

Brock, Richard Christie, Barbara Fried, David Glass, Sam Glucksberg, Robert Krauss, Thomas Ostrom, Stanley Schachter, Morris Stein, and Ladd Wheeler.

Stephanie Sommer, Susan Farber, and Dorothea Rolli, often with no advance warning, managed to meet impossible typing deadlines while still remaining friendly. We thank them for their forbearance and their cheerful competence. Finally, we wish to thank the 4,968 subjects who contributed from 20 seconds to two hours of their time to provide the evidence on which this book is based.

Bibb Latané
John M. Darley

CONTENTS

1 THE THREEFOLD CORD

> Two are better than one; because they have a good reward for their labor. For if they fall, the one will lift up his fellow: but woe to him that is alone when he falleth; for he hath not another to help him up. Again, if two lie together, then they have heat: but how can one be warm alone? And if one prevail against him, two shall withstand him; and a three-fold cord is not easily broken.
> *Ecclesiastes* 4:9–12.

In one of the oldest theories of social attraction extant, the Preacher suggests that men are bonded together in societies by a threefold cord consisting of succor, warmth, and mutual defense. Later theorists have agreed with him. Indeed, some have suggested that the whole structure of human society as well as the reason for its existence rests upon the fact that individuals are better off when they are in the company of others than when they are alone. Although people still seem prone to lie down together and produce heat, contemporary observers express concern over whether they are still willing to lift up their fallen fellow or to come to the defense of the victim of an attack. In part, this concern stems from the general feeling that present-day society is fragmented, that compassion is disappearing, that old moralities are crumbling, that man is becoming a machine. In part, it stems from more concrete evidence:

> Kitty Genovese is set upon by a maniac as she returns home from work at 3 A.M. Thirty-eight of her neighbors in Kew Gardens come to their windows when she cries out in terror; none come to her assistance even though her stalker takes over half an hour to murder her. No one even so much as calls the police. She dies.

1

Andrew Mormille is stabbed in the stomach as he rides the *A* train home in Manhattan. Eleven other riders watch the 17-year-old boy as he bleeds to death; none come to his assistance even though his attackers have left the car. He dies.

An 18-year-old switchboard operator, alone in her office in the Bronx, is raped and beaten. Escaping momentarily, she runs naked and bleeding to the street, screaming for help. A crowd of 40 passersby gathers and watches as, in broad daylight, the rapist tries to drag her back upstairs; no one interferes. Finally, two policemen happen by and arrest her assailant.

Over the past five years, dozens of such incidents have occurred and have received widespread publicity. The Kitty Genovese case itself has been the basis for television news specials, special issues of magazines, an Off Broadway play, a book, and innumerable columns, sermons, etc. The Andrew Mormille case became a feature movie, "The Incident." Both cases have had enormous national impact on our consciousness and on our conscience.

As with all frightening events that shake our conceptions of human nature, explanations for these terrifying failures of human compassion have been eagerly sought. Many explanations have been put forward: "I would assign this to the effect of the megalopolis in which we live, which makes closeness very difficult and leads to the alienation of the individual from the group," contributed a psychoanalyst. "A disaster syndrome," explained a sociologist, "that shook the sense of safety and sureness of the individuals involved and caused psychological withdrawal from the event by ignoring it." "Apathy," others claim. "Indifference." "The gratification of unconscious sadistic impulses." "Lack of concern for our fellow men." "The Cold Society." These and other explanations applied to the shocking failure of bystanders to intervene in emergencies suggest that we no longer care about the fate of our neighbors.

A. M. Rosenthal, who as Metropolitan Editor of the *New York Times* developed the Kitty Genovese story, describes expert reactions to the case in his interesting book, *Thirty-Eight Witnesses:*

I am fascinated, now, by the threads that ran through the "reaction" from our professional sources, that day and in the days that followed. The reaction of almost every one of these social physicians was to admit total failure on their part to understand, or to look for a comforting bit of jargon, or to reach out for a target—metropolitan living, or fear of the police, or TV sadism.

Everybody used a word that had been in the headline in the story—apathy.

Experts in human behavior, such as psychiatrists and sociologists, our story found, seemed as hard put as anyone else to explain the inaction of the witnesses. One sociologist called it "non-rational behavior."

A professor at the Downstate Medical Center of New York State University said the incident "goes to the heart of whether this is a community or a jungle." He suggested that when members of a society failed to defend each other they came close to being partners in crime. Then he added that he felt the incident was "atypical" and that New York as a community could not be condemned.

A psychiatrist called the incident typical—not atypical—of middle-class groups in a city like New York. "They have a nice life and what happens in the street, the life of the city itself, is a different matter." The same psychiatrist, Dr. George Serban, said that there was a constant feeling in New York that society was unjust and that that might be the explanation.

"It's the air of all New York, the air of injustice," he said. "The feeling that you might get hurt if you act and that whatever you do, you will be the one to suffer."

My own favorite comment came from the theologian who said that he could not understand it, that perhaps "depersonalizing" in New York had gone farther than he thought. Then he added, in monumental, total unconsciousness of irony: "Don't quote me."

Some time later, a psychiatrist, Dr. Ralph S. Banay, told a symposium on violence conducted by the Medical Correctional Association that a confusion of fantasy with reality, fed by an endless stream of TV violence, was in part responsible for the fact that the witnesses to Miss Genovese's murder had turned away. "We underestimate the damage that these accumulated images do to the brain," he said. "The immediate effect can be delusional, equivalent to a sort of posthypnotic suggestion."

Dr. Banay suggested that the murder vicariously gratified the sadistic impulses of those who witnessed it. "They were deaf, paralyzed, hypnotized with excitation," he said. "Fascinated by the drama, by the action, and yet not entirely sure that what was taking place was actually happening."

Explanations for similar incidents suggest that people have grown increasingly alienated from the norms and institutions of our Judaeo-

Christian society. They imply the emergence of a new kind of man, *"homo urbanis,"* who has adapted to the pressures caused by the increasing urbanization of life by turning other people into objects, by losing human feeling for them, and by rejecting the moral imperative to help another in distress. Nothing seems left of the Biblical threefold cord except uneasy alliances of self-gratification.

But can all this be so? We think not. Although it is unquestionably true that the witnesses in these incidents did nothing to save the victims, "apathy," "indifference," and "unconcern" are not entirely accurate descriptions of their reactions. The 38 witnesses of Kitty Genovese's murder did not merely look at the scene once and then ignore it. Instead they continued to stare out of their windows at what was going on. Caught, fascinated, distressed, unwilling to act but unable to turn away, their behavior was neither helpful nor heroic; but it was not indifferent or apathetic either.

Actually, it was like crowd behavior in many other emergency situations: car accidents, drownings, fires, and attempted suicides all attract substantial numbers of people who watch the drama in helpless fascination without getting directly involved in the action. Are these people alienated and indifferent? Are the rest of us? We think not. It seems only yesterday we were being called overconforming. But why, then, don't we act?

But, of course, people sometimes do act. People often help others, even at great personal risk to themselves. For every "apathy" story, one of outright heroism could be cited. In addition, "apathy" stories, being dramatic, get into the newspapers. Cases of intervention, where witnesses do call the police, being more routine, do not. It is a mistake to get trapped by the wave of publicity and discussion surrounding incidents in which help was not forthcoming into believing that help never comes. The threefold cord has not been completely severed. Altruism is not completely dead. People sometimes help and sometimes don't. What determines when help will be given?

Altruism presents a problem for psychology. Altruistic behavior may please us as people, but it embarrasses traditional theories of psychology that are founded on the assumption that man is moved only by considerations of reward and punishment. The hedonistic tone of this traditional reinforcement theory is at variance with the simple observed fact that people do help others in circumstances in which there seem to be no gains, and even considerable risk, for doing so.

Reinforcement theory's traditional resolution of this dilemma is to postulate that individuals do in fact get rewards, or at least avoid punishments, for acting altruistically. The sight of a person in distress arouses sympathetic or empathic feelings in an observer—"primitive passive sympathy," as McDougall described it—and the observer, in helping the victim, helps himself. He is not so much motivated to relieve the victim's distress as he is to alleviate his own empathic suffering and to feel the anticipated empathic pleasure he can take at another's joy and relief at receiving help. Just as we feel good along with the characters who come to a happy ending in a novel, we may anticipate feeling good by helping to cause a happy ending in real life.

These explanations for altruism are based on our identification with or sympathy for an individual in distress. Another possible explanation is that we may actually be guided less by our feelings toward the victim than by our desire to look good in front of other people. These others may be physically present at the scene or they may be psychologically present in the sense that their approval has been necessary in the past and their ideal that helping others is good has been accepted by the person being altruistic. This explanation, which also preserves a hedonistic account of altruism, postulates norms which the individual must learn to follow. There is a norm, according to this view, to help other individuals in distress. If a properly socialized individual of a culture violates the helping norm he subjects himself to negative consequences which punish him for his failure to help. As with the "shared suffering" explanation, the onlooker acts altruistically because of the negative consequences of doing otherwise. In this case, the negative consequences are anticipated in the future rather than felt in the immediate present.

Various theories suggest various processes by which norms are enforced. For Freudians, rules originally enforced externally, largely by the parents, become internalized in the process of development to form the superego. Violation of these rules leads to feelings of guilt, which are self-punishing. Other theorists locate the rules and their enforcing mechanisms in other members of the society in which the individual lives. They assert that norms are enforced by the threat of the disapproval of other onlookers and also, perhaps, by the more concrete negative consequences that may stem from this disapproval.

Many of the explanations for bystander inaction in emergencies imply either that our feelings of compassion for each other or our willingness to adhere to social norms of helping have eroded and become impotent as forces towards helping. We have become apathetic toward the distress of others, indifferent as to their fate; we have lost our ability to feel empathy, compassion, or sympathy for others—so runs one line of explanation. We have become alienated from society, anomic, unwilling to share its values or follow its dictates except under pressure; we are moral dropouts—so runs a different line of explanation. Both of these explanations share one thing in common: they attribute increasing bystander inaction to a change in the strength of basic motives underlying altruism. Is this necessarily so? We think not. Changes in frequency of a behavior do not necessarily imply a change in the motives underlying that behavior.

It seems to us that many discussions of altruism have confused two basic questions, and that understanding can more profitably be advanced if these questions are separated. The first question, put most generally, asks, "What is the underlying force in mankind toward altruism?" or "What motivates helping?" The second question is more specific: "What determines in a particular situation whether one person will help another?" The first question is a general one, of enormous social interest and importance, and of a semiphilosophic nature. It probably will never be completely answered by reference to data. The second question is more specific, more mundane, more amenable to research analysis.

There is no reason to expect that principles used in answering the first question should also be important or even have much bearing on the second. It is possible, for example, that norms provide a general predisposition to help other people, but that whether someone will help in a particular situation is dependent upon other factors. These factors may involve the interpretations people make about what is happening or they may involve the rewards and costs that are associated with various courses of action. If we can get some idea of the kinds of factors which influence a person's decision to help or not to help, we may also arrive at a position to understand his motives.

2 HELPING IN
NONEMERGENCY SITUATIONS

The problem of altruism is not restricted to emergencies. People are dependent on each other for many things. In small matters as well as large, people need and ask for but do not always receive help from others. In this chapter we shall report a number of experiments dealing with helping in nonemergency situations. An understanding of helping in these simple situations will be useful when we turn to a consideration of emergencies.

All the experiments we shall report in this chapter were conducted in field settings. They involved a conscious attempt to get out of the laboratory. A major difficulty with laboratory studies of helping is that they are hard to relate to real-life situations. On the one hand, subjects are under unusual pressures in the laboratory. They are known by name to the experimenter and sometimes to other subjects and they may be eager to gain favorable evaluations from them. They have been pulled out of their daily routine and are shorn of many of their usual defenses. They cannot easily leave the situation and they may find it hard simply to ignore a request. These heightened pressures and lowered defenses may make the laboratory subject much more vulnerable to a request for help than the man on the street.

Furthermore, laboratory experiments often have an "as if" quality about them. If subjects know that they are participating in an experiment, they may react not to what they see, but to what they think the experiment is about. Anxious to make a favorable impression, they may be willing to act quite unnaturally in order to appear normal. They are likely to playact. These forces may be especially strong in situations where norms are involved. Self-conscious and apprehensive about being evaluated, laboratory subjects may make an unusual attempt to behave normatively.

A third dissimilarity between laboratory helping situations and life is that in order to make a request for help believable in its laboratory context and in order to increase the measurement utility of the response, subjects may be faced with rather unusual demands. "How many hours are you willing to spend in sensory deprivation?" "Will you help stack these papers?" "How many letters will you address for 'Save the Redwoods'?" Although laboratory experiments constitute an invaluable technique for testing theoretical derivations, they may not tell us much about the determinants of helping in everyday situations.

EXPERIMENT 1. TYPE AND MANNER OF REQUEST *

In this experiment, students in introductory social psychology courses at Columbia University went out on the streets of New York and asked 1,520 passersby one of a variety of simple requests. They asked for different kinds of help and they asked for it in different ways. The varying responses to their requests provide a first approximation to questions about the prevalence of altruistic compliance and the parameters influencing it.

Students, for the most part relatively clean-cut, well-dressed male undergraduates, were sent out into the streets of Manhattan in the Springs of 1966–68. They were rather a diverse group. Ranging in age from 18 to 50, they included hippies, housewives, Jews, jocks, Negroes, Orientals, Europeans, Latin Americans, ROTC students, radicals, nurses, and models as well as a few typical college students. There were undoubtedly differences in the approach, accent, intonation, and eye contact employed by the students.

Students participated in the study as part of a class assignment. For the most part they seemed interested in the study and found the task rather easy. The few who felt too embarrassed to "beg on the streets" were allowed to take other projects. A number of checks supported the veracity and accuracy of the students' reports of their results;

---

* Experiments 1–3 are reported somewhat more fully in Latané, B. Field studies in altruistic compliance. *Representative Research in Social Psychology,* 1970, *1.*

the number of fabricated cases was almost certainly less than 5 percent of the total.

The subjects they contacted were passersby on the streets and in public places. Students avoided the Columbia area, but spread out over the East and West sides and Greenwich Village. Of the people they asked to help, 61 percent were male, 47 percent were alone, and 70 percent were moving at the time of the request. Thirty percent of the requests were made in indoor locations such as subway stations and railway terminals and 70 percent were made outdoors. Sixty percent of the requests were made in fairly crowded surroundings, with five or more people within about 30 feet.

Students were asked to be as unselective as possible about whom to "hit"; several devices were used to prevent systematic sampling of subjects. Although there probably was a tendency to avoid the most seedy or most threatening prospective donors, the sample is not too unrepresentative of those New Yorkers who can be found in public places. After selecting a potential subject, students covertly consulted a previously shuffled deck of data-recording cards to determine which kind of assistance to ask for. This procedure ensured the random assignment of subjects to experimental conditions, thus preventing the experimenter from unconsciously biasing the selection of subjects.

Type of request. The first experimental variation consisted simply of the kind of help the students asked for. Students asked for three kinds of minor assistance (time, directions, or change), for money, or for the subject's name. The results are shown in Table 1.

The type of request made a major difference in the likelihood of receiving help. Students were very successful in getting minor assistance. Only 15 percent of the subjects refused to give the time and few of these made an overt refusal; most simply ignored the request (some, possibly, because they genuinely did not hear it). When asked for directions, subjects were again very helpful. Few refused the request, most gave adequate directions, and some went to great lengths to do so, sometimes going several blocks out of their way to show the correct route. Almost three-quarters of those asked for change made at least a sincere attempt to find it, going through their pockets or stopping somebody else to get it. It is possible that some of the refusals were from people who knew without looking that they had no change.

Students were much less successful when they asked for the subject's name. Fewer than 40 percent of those who were asked gave their

TABLE 1
Frequency of Response to Different Requests

"Excuse me, I wonder if you could . . .	Number asked	Percent helping
a. tell me what time it is?"	92	85$_a$
b. tell me how to get to Times Square?"	90	84$_a$
c. give me change of a quarter?"	90	73$_a$
d. tell me what your name is?"	277	39$_b$
e. give me a dime?"	284	34$_b$

Note: All conditions except those which share the same subscript are significantly different, $p < .05$. This means that the probability that differences could have occurred by chance alone is less than five times in a hundred, and consequently, that they are most likely due to the experimental manipulations.

names, and then, usually, they gave only their first names. Subjects usually seemed surprised when asked for their names, and the students reported that those who gave them often seemed to do it out of sheer reflex. Subjects often inquired, "Why do you want to know?" or "What's it to you?"

The request for a dime led to the least success. Only one-third of the subjects gave it, or made an apparently sincere effort to find a dime. Although this rate of response was relatively low, it is probably considerably higher than that enjoyed by the average panhandler, bum, or derelict. College students obviously do not need money so much as the average panhandler, but then, they are generally cleaner cut, better dressed, and more prosperous looking. And it may be that subjects assumed they would spend the money to better purpose.

Manner of request. Although the bald request for a dime worked in only one-third of the cases, requests including more information were markedly more successful. Table 2 lists five variations on the request for a dime and the response each achieved. If the student gave his name before asking for a dime, he had about a 50-50 chance of getting help, and if he claimed that he needed to make a telephone call, or that he had lost his wallet, he was helped over two-thirds of the time.

Information preceding the request had as striking an effect when students asked for names. Students who asked simply, "Could you tell me what your name is?" were answered 39 percent of the time. When

TABLE 2

Frequency of Response as a Function of Manner of Request

Manner of request	Number asked	Percent helping
a. "Excuse me, I wonder if you could give me a dime?"	284	34_a
b. "Excuse me, I wonder if you could give me a dime? I've spent all my money."	108	38_{ab}
c. "Excuse me, I wonder if you could tell me what time it is? . . . and could you give me a dime?"	146	43_{ab}
d. "Excuse me, my name is _____. I wonder if you could give me a dime?"	150	49_b
e. "Excuse me, I wonder if you could give me a dime? I need to make a telephone call."	111	64_c
f. "Excuse me, I wonder if you could give me a dime? My wallet has been stolen."	108	72_c
a. "Excuse me, could you tell me what your name is?"	277	39_a
b. "Excuse me, my name is _____. Could you tell me what your name is?"	64	59_b

Note: All conditions except those which share the same subscript are significantly different, $p < .05$.

they said, "Excuse me, my name is _____. Could you tell me what your name is?" 59 percent of the 64 asked gave their names ($p < .01$).

The manner of request had clear effects on the likelihood of response; the reasons for these effects are less clear. It is possible that the addition of information gave the subject more justification for donating the money, it may be that the information served mainly to reduce the strangeness or suspiciousness of the request, or it may be that the information was effective largely because it tended to create a closer bond between the requester and the subject. The present data do not allow a choice among these or other alternatives.

Situational determinants. Whether the subject was moving or was indoors or out at the time of the request had no effect on his likelihood of giving minor forms of assistance. These variables had a moderate effect on his likelihood of giving a dime; 47 percent of moving subjects and 58 percent of stationary subjects gave ($p < .01$) and 49 percent of subjects contacted outdoors and 54 percent of indoor subjects gave (n.s.). These variables had a large effect on the likelihood of giving a name: 29 percent of moving and 63 percent of stationary subjects ($p < .01$), 37 percent of outdoor and 54 percent of indoor subjects ($p < .05$) gave their names.

Sex of subject and of requester. Sex had no effect on giving minor assistance. Sex affected the request for a dime: female requesters were helped by 58 percent of the subjects while males were helped by only 46 percent ($p < .02$). Sex of the subjects had no effect on the request for a dime (but see Experiment 2). Sex also had a large effect on the request for a name, but a different pattern of results emerged. Females were more likely to receive an answer—but only if the subject were male. Sixty-eight percent of male subjects gave their name to a female; other sex pairings achieved response rates of 37–39 percent ($p < .01$). The girls making these requests were all at least moderately attractive and the males they approached ranged in age from 15 to 80.

DISCUSSION

Sex, movement, and location had different effects on the requests for minor assistance, money, and names. The lack of relationship between these variables and the giving of minor assistance may simply reflect a ceiling effect: it may be that 15 percent of Manhattanites are chronic grouches who wouldn't give the time of day even to Snow White. The differences between names and dimes are less easy to explain. The request for a name may have a different meaning than the request for a dime; it is certainly unclear whether giving someone your name is an act of charity. Perhaps the major question facing subjects asked for their names was how to extricate themselves from a strange situation without giving undue offense.

The results of this experiment suggest that people, even New

Yorkers, are surprisingly willing to comply with a stranger's request. They also imply that circumstances greatly influence how a person responds to a request for help. The kind of assistance requested and the way in which the request was made had strong effects. The sex differences suggest that the kind of person making the request is also important. Experiment 2 further explored this issue.

EXPERIMENT 2. NUMBER AND SEX OF REQUESTERS

If a person, for the same cost, can help two people rather than just one, will he be more likely to help? To answer this question, 11 male and eight female students asked 2,091 passersby for twenty cents for the subway. They asked either alone, in pairs, or in trios. The pairs were composed either of one male and one female, of two males, or of two females. The trios consisted of two males and one female.

The form of request was standard in all cases: "Excuse me, could you help me (us)? I (we) have to get downtown and need twenty cents for the subway." Since it was impossible to randomly assign subjects by the technique used in Experiment 1, a new procedure was devised. Students waited 20 seconds after recording the response to their previous request and then approached the next person to come into range. Students frequently alternated among the conditions. Table 3 presents their results.

TABLE 3
Frequency of Response as a Function of Number of Requesters

	Number asked	Percent helping
Alone	761	41
Pairs	1240	48
Trios	90	77

Note: All conditions are significantly different, p < .05.

It appears as if people do respond to the number of requesters. Pairs were more likely to receive help than were single students and trios received the most help. This conclusion must be strongly qualified, however, for the pattern of results depended strikingly upon the sex of the person making the request. The results are broken down in Table 4.

TABLE 4

Frequency of Response as a Function of Sex and Number of Requesters

Percent helping (N's in parentheses)

	Alone	Same sex pair	Mixed sex pair
Female asks	57 (319)$_b$	72 (240)$_a$	53 (323)$_b$
Male asks	30 (442)$_c$	25 (360)$_c$	50 (317)$_b$

Note: All conditions except those which share the same subscript are significantly different, p < .05. N is the number of subjects asked in each condition.

Females were almost twice as likely to receive help as males when alone and three times as likely when in same-sex pairs. There was no overlap between the sexes: the least successful female got help 54 percent of the time in these two conditions while the most successful male was helped only 40 percent of the time. This sex difference completely disappeared in the mixed-sex pairs and trios; it made no difference whether the male or the female made the request.

Females were more successful when they asked in same-sex pairs than when alone; males were slightly less. Males were more successful when accompanied by a female than when alone; females were slightly less successful when accompanied by a male. These results suggest that subjects responded to the pair as a unit and not just to the person making the request. They also suggest that if you (whether you are male or female) ever happen to need twenty cents for the subway, it would be a good idea to have a girl with you and a bad idea to have a man.

Number and sex of subjects. Eighty-three percent of the subjects were alone when they were asked and 17 percent were in pairs or in groups of three. Subjects were somewhat more likely to help if they were alone; 47 percent of single subjects and only 40 percent of subjects in groups of two or more gave help (p < .05).

In this experiment, unlike Experiment 1, the sex of the subject made a major difference in the likelihood of response. Overall, males were much more likely to help (52 percent) than were females (40 percent). There was, however, no interaction between the sex of the requester and the sex of the subject. These results are shown in Table 5.

It is interesting that those characteristics of requesters which made

TABLE 5
Frequency of Response by Sex of Subject and Sex of Requester

	Percent helping (N's in parentheses)	
	Female subject	Male subject
Female asks	54 (395)	68 (367)
Male asks	27 (437)	40 (505)

Note: All conditions are significantly different, $p < .05$.

them most likely to receive help (being female, being in a group), were the characteristics which made the subjects least likely to give help.

DISCUSSION

How can we account for the differences due to sex and number of requesters? One possibility is a "cost-effectiveness" explanation. The more you get in return for your money, the more likely you are to help. If it is gratitude you are seeking, you are more likely to get it from a group than from an individual. And you may feel that you make a bigger contribution to society or to your ego if you help a girl or a group rather than a single man.

A second explanation would emphasize what subjects assume about the motives and future behavior of the requester. As a subject you may be more likely to give money to a girl or to a group because you are less suspicious or afraid of them than of a single man, or less suspicious that the person is trying to con you, that he does not actually need the money, or that he is not just a well-dressed bum. You may be less afraid that you will make a fool of yourself, that the asker will try to take further advantage of you, or that he will snatch your purse or wallet as you try to help. In short, you may be more likely to think that a girl or a person in a group is decent and sincere than to believe those characteristics of one or two men.

This line of explanation assumes that the interpretation a person puts on an event will shape his reaction to it. If he arrives at a negative interpretation, or even, perhaps, if he is unsure what interpretation to arrive at, he will be less likely to help. Experiment 3 attempted to manipulate interpretation directly, but in a new kind of situation—one where the subject was offered a favor rather than asked for one.

EXPERIMENT 3. TAKING CANDY FROM STRANGERS

Mothers warn us never to take candy from a stranger. Our society also assumes that it is a lucky man who gets something for nothing. In order to see which of these policies people follow, two Columbia students, Toby Bonnett and Irene Willwerth, offered candy to 320 strangers on the streets of New York. They offered either a small piece of candy, a penny Hershey chocolate kiss wrapped in silver foil, or a larger piece of candy, a nickel Hershey chocolate bar. They offered the candy either alone or in a pair, with the two girls standing side-by-side. Finally, they offered the candy either by saying, "Would you like a Hershey bar (chocolate kiss)? It's a gift," or with an explanation: "Would you like a Hershey bar (chocolate kiss)? It's a free sample, compliments of the Hershey Company." Alternating experimental conditions, the girls approached the first person to step in a specified pavement square 20 seconds after their last request.

RESULTS

Forty-one percent of 160 people offered candy bars accepted; only 31 percent of those offered chocolate kisses did so ($p < .05$). Whether the girls offered the candy alone or together made little difference. Forty percent of the people approached together and 33 percent of those approached alone accepted (this difference in percentages is not statistically significant [n.s.] and therefore is most likely due to chance). The rationale for the gift made a large difference. Those who were given no excuse other than "It's a gift" accepted 27 percent of the time. Those who were told that "It's a free sample, compliments of the Hershey Company," accepted 46 percent of the time ($p < .0005$). There were no interactions among these variables.

Many of the people who refused the candy seemed to do so out of fear. Some people said, "Please!" or "Get away"; some simply stared; and others walked on without even listening to the offer. Other people gave legitimate reasons for declining the candy. Some were fat and said, "I'm dieting," or "It's fattening." Others were allergic or didn't like chocolate. A few were already eating ice cream or candy. One man said he had false teeth and would have to take them out to wash them if he ate the chocolate.

Of those who accepted the candy, some just took it and walked on without even a smile or nod. But most were friendly. "You mean you're giving it to me?" "Don't you want it?" "Thank you, I have a sweet tooth." "There are a few nice people left." "A free sample! I'll take anything for free!" In some cases, the girls got similar reactions whether the people refused the candy or not. Either they smiled, thought it was a joke, did not understand English, or asked the price.

The offer of free candy is not an everyday event in New York City. It tends to be greeted with suspicion. Everyone has heard stories of real-life witches who poison Halloween candy. It is perhaps surprising that so many people accepted. Part of the reason may have been that the candy was offered by attractive, wholesome-looking girls. In a pilot study in which Columbia men offered Hershey bars, only 19 out of 100 accepted. You may feel hostile and suspicious if someone offers you a free gift for no good reason—but a free sample distributed as a public relations gesture for commercial purposes provides reason enough. People may also be reluctant to accept favors which they cannot reciprocate. Doing so would set up a state of inequity, a need to return the favor, an undischarged obligation. Accepting a free sample, however, implies no obligation. The donor is rewarded if you try his product.

3 NORMS AND BEHAVIOR

Why do people give money to a stranger? Why are they more likely to do so under some conditions than under others? Some theorists would answer both questions with one word—"norms." We help others because there are norms that say we should do so. We help more in some situations than in others because norms differ from one situation to another. When we are faced with a dependent person, the "social responsibility" norms will operate. When we have received a favor, we are bound by the "reciprocity" norm. When there is an overly great disparity in wealth, we may feel uncomfortable because of the "equal outcomes" norm.

A second reason why norms may have different effects from one situation to another is that they may vary in "salience." A number of experimenters have shown that if one person does something, another person, seeing him, may be more likely to do that thing also. According to one common explanation for such effects, the model, by his behavior, increases the salience of one or another norm for the observer, who is consequently more likely to obey this norm.

There may be considerable validity in such norm-centered accounts of behavior, but there are also difficulties. A major difficulty with norms is that they seem, at least in simple statement, contradictory. In our society we are told to "do unto others as you would have them do unto you." We usually interpret this to mean that we should help others. Yet we are also taught "don't take candy from a stranger," or more generally, do not accept help from others. If we won't accept help from others, then the Golden Rule becomes somewhat ambiguous. This normative ambivalence toward helping and being helped is well illustrated by

Adam Lindsay Gordon in his forgotten classic, *Ye Wearie Wayfarer*.
Gordon exhorts us:

> Question not but live and labour
> Till yon goal be won,
> Helping every feeble neighbor,
> Seeking help from none.
>
> Life is mostly froth and bubble
> Two things stand like stone
> Kindness in another's trouble
> Courage in your own.

Norms tell us we should not ask for help; they also suggest that we should not offer it at too great cost to ourselves. It would be irrational, unbusinesslike, un-American to do so. As Mr. Deeds discovered to his chagrin, the overly generous philanthropist may be looked on with suspicion and disapproval, if not outright hostility. As a modern example of this, a poor man recently found a sack of money that had fallen from a Brinks truck. Honest, he returned the money to Brinks, who were quite startled, as they had not yet discovered the loss. Although publicized as a hero, he received scores of threatening and vilifying calls and letters castigating him for being a fool and exhorting him to look out for himself in the future.

A final way in which norms of helping conflict with other norms is that we are taught to respect the privacy of others. If you intrude into another's distress, even with the best of intentions, you may find yourself resented and reviled. "Mind your own business," you may be told, "Don't stick your nose in somebody else's mess." The Bible, as always, has the more elegant way of expressing this point. "He that passeth by, and meddleth with strife belonging not to him, is like one that taketh a dog by the ears," Proverbs 26:17.

Norms, then, seem to contradict one another. The injunction to help other people is qualified by strictures not to accept help, to look out for yourself, and not to meddle in other people's business. In any specific situation it is hard to see how norms will be of much help to an undecided bystander.

A second problem with norms is that, even though contradictory, they are usually stated in only the most vague and general way. There are probably good reasons why this is so. To specify norms in sufficient detail to allow them to be useful guides in specific situations would require an elaborately qualified, lengthily stated, integrated set of rules covering a wide variety of situations, many of which will arise only infrequently. It is difficult to imagine an embattled bystander watching an act or hearing a request, wondering what to do, and leafing through his mental rule book to exclaim, "Aha! That reminds me! Section 34.62b just fits this case!"

These problems seriously diminish the value of norms as a scientific construct in explaining helping behavior. Since norms are so many and so vague, they can be used to explain almost any pattern of behavior. They can explain why people were so willing to give the correct time, change of a quarter, or directions. There is a norm to "help thy neighbor." They can explain why people were less likely to give money. There is a norm to "look out for yourself." They can explain why people often refused to give their names. There is a norm to "protect your privacy." Females were more successful in getting money than males because there is a norm to help the weak. Males were more likely to give their names to females because there is a norm to be gallant. Couples were . . . but stop. We are citing one new norm to explain each successive comparison. To continue in this fashion would be to do nothing more than to give ad hoc explanations for results that we could not have predicted in advance. Norms can explain so much that they really explain very little. By being able to explain anything, they really explain nothing.

Norms do not seem very useful to the scientist, because they are so vague, unspecific, and conflicting. For the same reasons, they may be of little use to an individual trying to decide what course of action to take in a specific situation. It is possible that norms are relatively unimportant determinants of behavior, a possibility that is supported by the next two experiments.

EXPERIMENT 4. LOST IN THE SUBWAY

The next study took place in the subways of New York City and was done by Harvey Allen as a Ph.D. dissertation at New York University. The situation he used was a prearranged asking for information between two experimenters. A subway rider was selected as an (unwitting) subject. One experimenter stood or sat near him. The other experimenter, in the guise of a bewildered looking individual, approached and asked whether the subway was going uptown or downtown. The experimenter —or bystander—gave the wrong answer—if the subway was going uptown, he replied "downtown" and vice versa. The dilemma for the subject is: should he give the right information, correcting the bystander, or not?

The dependent measure of the study was whether the bystander corrected the misinformer. In the first study, Allen varied the direction in which the original request for information was aimed. In one condition, the request was aimed at the subject, in a second condition, the question was aimed at both bystanders, and in the third condition, the misinformer-to-be was directly addressed. These variations had major effects (Table 6).

TABLE 6
Percent Correcting Misinformation

Direction of question	N	Percent correcting
To misinformer	30	27_a
To group	80	50_a
To subject	30	93_b

Note: All conditions except those which share the same subscript are significantly different, $p < .05$.

When the misinformer cut in to answer the question asked of the naive subject, subjects almost always corrected him and did so immediately, impatiently, and indignantly. When the original question was addressed generally toward the two-person group, subjects corrected considerably less frequently. Finally, when the question was directed at the misinformer, subjects corrected least frequently of all. Even though norms governing response should be fairly constant, situational variables can have a strong effect on the frequency of help.

Allen's second study demonstrates that people behave in accordance with their estimates of the cost to themselves for doing so. Again someone asked for directions and was misinformed, thus putting pressure on the naive subject to correct him. In this experiment, the question was always aimed at both the confederate and the naive bystander since that had given nearest to a 50-50 split of responding in the previous study.

But this time, the misinformer-to-be first created a character for himself. He sat with his legs stretched in front of him in the subway car and when his confederate walked past him and stumbled over his feet, the misinformer-to-be responded in one of three ways: by doing nothing, by looking up from his muscle-building magazine and shouting threats of physical harm at the hapless stumbler, or by making embarrassing comments about him. In the last two conditions, therefore, the misinformer-to-be established that he was ready to resort to physical violence or noisy vituperation when crossed. When he subsequently misinformed the direction-seeker, he presented a rather acute dilemma for the real subject. To offer the correct information required contradicting the misinformer, a man who had demonstrated he might react badly to correction. In a fourth condition, the misinformer gave a tentative answer to the request for directions: "Uptown, but I'm not sure," making it clear that he was unsure about his answer. This made it seem unlikely that he would confront a person who corrected him.

The effects are quite clear and much as one would expect them to be. (Table 7.)

TABLE 7
Percent Correcting Misinformation

Degree of threat	N	Percent correcting
Physical threat	50	16$_a$
Embarrassment	50	28$_a$
Control	80	50$_b$
Reduced embarrassment	50	82$_c$

Note: All conditions except those which share the same subscript are significantly different, p < .05.

The subject was most reluctant to correct the physically threatening person and least reluctant to correct the tentatively answering person. The correction rate for the potentially embarrassing person fell in between. Clearly subjects calculated the cost of help and modified their behavior accordingly.

If the subject had not corrected the misinformer after a fixed period of time (usually 30 seconds) the misinformer walked away out of ear shot, thus eliminating whatever reluctance the subject might have felt to contradict him. Among subjects who had failed to correct by the time the misinformer had left, correction was *still* less likely when the misinformer had established a threatening or embarrassing character for himself.

Subjects ranged in age from teen-agers to over sixty, were of both sexes, and of a wide variety of ethnic affiliations. The sex of the subject, his age, or any other demographic variable were not significantly related to his helping behavior.

In both these studies, differences between conditions showed up even though norms for helping should have been equally strong. Allen's third study tried to vary norms directly by varying the character of the direction-asker, who was later to be misinformed. In one condition he was dressed as an obvious tourist, carrying a travel bag with stickers from the Midwest, and dressed in a semiwestern hat. This should add norms about helping strangers to the situation. In a second condition, the future direction-asker established that he was himself a helping person. A female confederate (by this time you must have the feeling that roughly half of the population of New York served as confederates —Allen had the same feeling when he paid them), heavily laden with packages, dropped them. The future direction-asker helped her to pick them up, hopefully engaging norms of reciprocity and modelling a help-giving act. The third condition was a control condition; no particular character was established for the direction-asker.

Although the effects were in the direction one might anticipate, no significant differences were found. In a situation in which it seems plausible to assume that norms of helping strangers and norms connected with reciprocity of helping actions were aroused, no significant differences were produced in helping behavior.

EXPERIMENT 5. TO FRISBEE OR NOT TO FRISBEE

You are probably familiar with the frisbee, or pluto platter, that appears on college campuses in the spring. It is a circular, pie plate-like disc which, when propelled by a expert, can be made to fly or float through the air in complex and graceful arcs. The amount of time college students take off from more scholarly activities to devote to the study of frisbees suggests that the activity is pleasurable and even fascinating. In a study conducted in a senior social psychology seminar at New

York University, Sheri Turtletaub and Harriet Ortman cleverly capitalized on this fascination to study the promotion of interaction among groups of strangers. They were concerned with factors promoting interaction among previously nonorganized groups in public places. Most specifically, their task was to turn the Grand Central Station waiting room into a frenzy of flying frisbees.

A girl sat on a bench in the waiting room at Grand Central. Soon another girl sat on a bench facing her. They recognized each other and began a conversation. One girl had been shopping and announced that she had just bought a frisbee. The other girl asked to see it and the first girl threw it to her. They then began to toss it back and forth. Apparently by accident, the frisbee was thrown to a third person and the reaction of this third person (an experimental confederate), was the independent variable of the study. That person either enthusiastically joined in throwing the frisbee or accused the two girls of being childish and dangerous, and kicked the frisbee back across the gap.

Whichever of these two variations occurred, the two girls continued throwing the frisbee back and forth and eventually threw it to one of the real bystanders seated on the benches. They continued this until all the bystandars on the two facing benches had been tried. A bystander was counted as participating in the activity if he returned the frisbee at least twice. The percentage of bystanders who joined in the frisbee fest was the dependent measure of the study.

When the experimental confederate joined in the play, the other spectators were extremely likely to do so also. The average percentage of participation over four cases was 86 percent and people often came from other areas of the waiting room to participate. Indeed in this condition the problem was not to start interaction but to terminate it, so the experimenters could leave for the next waiting room and run further tests.

On the other hand, if the confederate refused to play and instead disapproved of the girl's activity, no other bystander ever joined in the action. Instead, people sitting nearby would frequently get up and move to other seats to avoid being thrown a frisbee, muttering their disapproval while doing so.

The girls went on to run further tests in an attempt to determine which features of the confederate's behavior were critical. In one condition, the confederate returned the frisbee to the two girls without commenting or otherwise joining in the action. A high percentage, 74 percent, of bystanders participated, not significantly different from the positive participation condition. In another condition, the confederate did not join in the action but allowed the frisbee to bounce off her accidentally and be retrieved by one of the two original girls. Under these circumstances, too, other bystanders participated at a high rate. The confederate who was a model for inaction failed to inhibit participation by other bystanders.

These results suggest that what the confederate did was less important than what the confederate said. Interaction was significantly inhibited only when the confederate loudly denounced the frisbee throwers. The results also suggest a normative analysis. When certain norms are made salient, they inhibit action. The experimenters ran other tests to distinguish exactly which norms were operative in the situation. In these further conditions, the confederate carefully confined her negative comments to an appeal to one norm. In one situation, she cited the danger to others that was caused by throwing the frisbee and in another she accused the participants of indulging in childish behavior.

Both types of sanctions inhibited action about equally. The overall percentage of participation was about 27 percent. However, the girls did a final manipulation which calls a norm-centered account into question: either the confederate stayed to watch the frisbee players after she gave her sanctions or she immediately left the waiting room. When the confederate stayed, play was greatly inhibited. When she left, the percentage of bystanders participating rose to near its original rate. The sanctioning speech by itself did not inhibit play; it required the sanctioning speech *plus* the confederate's continued presence.

It might be argued that the continued presence of the sanctioning individual made the norm that she had evoked more salient and thus more inhibitory. This, we think, stretches the meaning of the word salience. Even when the denouncer left, she did so only after upbraiding the frisbee players. Obviously the norms she cited were salient to bystanders, in that they were forcefully brought to their attention. However, the bystanders still participated. Our explanation of the result ignores norms. It seems reasonable that the bystanders simply considered the costs of participating. When the spoilsport confederate stayed around, it was possible that she might yell at other bystanders who participated, call the police, or otherwise punish or embarrass the participants.

Norms, then, do not seem to provide satisfactory answers to why people act or fail to act in specific situations. Norms are contradictory, vague, and do not seem to be effective guides to behavior. And yet, they clearly exist. People talk about them. They use them to explain their own behavior and to castigate others if they fail to live up to them.

Children learn norms. They receive them as exhortations from parents, teachers, peers, and preachers. Embarrassingly, they often take them seriously. "I know you want to do what we taught you and help the poor, but you can't give that man all your piggy bank money. He's a drunk." Very few parents have not been confronted with a child's awkward but zealous application of an exhortation, which they have thereupon been forced to contradict. So a child learns an elaborate set of norms, but he also learns a set of behaviors that are relatively independent of these norms.

Like the King of England, norms may reign, but not rule. That is, they may exist, but have so little application to the complex real-life situations in which ethical considerations arise as not to be useful in explaining the actual variations in help-giving.

Finally, norms exist as a sort of nominal theory of behavior. They are an easy and socially acceptable after-the-fact explanation for one's actions even though never considered in deciding what to do. They are particularly useful in cases in which some of the actual determinants of behavior are not immediately accessible to awareness. In later chapters, we will show that bystanders to emergencies are affected in several ways by the presence of other bystanders, but that they seem to be unaware of this fact. Instead, they give normative accounts of their behavior, because this is the way that it is appropriate to talk in these circumstances.

In various ways, then, the fact that norms exist does not require that they function as causes of behavior, nor that a norm-centered explanation of helping behavior is scientifically useful.

The same criticisms may be marshalled against feelings of compassion or empathy as explanations for specific helping acts. As with norms, they may provide an overall predisposition to help or they may provide post hoc explanations for why we have acted in a certain way. As with norms, however, this does not mean that a feeling of compassion, or a wave of empathy, is either necessary or sufficient to produce helping behavior.

What then, does cause a person to help in a given emergency? We think the answer lies in a process analysis of what a person must think and do if he is to help another. Specifically, we think that before a person can decide what to do in a given situation, he must come to some interpretation of the situation, some evaluation of the nature of the situation confronting him, some conclusion about the motives of the other actors, and some conception of the possibilities inherent in the situation and what various courses of action might lead to. Once the person has come to an interpretation (whether it be correct or incorrect), he will act in terms of the various rewards and costs associated with the alternative courses of action available to him as *he sees them.*

We suspect that the major variance in behavior in helping situations will be determined by the various conclusions and interpretations each person makes and the various rewards and costs he sees, rather than by his overall willingness to adhere to social norms or to act generously or compassionately.

We suspect that the modern failure of bystanders to intervene in emergencies reflects modern influences on the ways people interpret situations and modern reward and cost structures, rather than a lessened tendency to follow moral norms or a lessened degree of compassion. Alienation from social norms or apathy about the fate of others may be oversimplified and therefore incorrect explanations for the unresponsive bystander. The answer may instead lie in the various decisions the bystander must make before he intervenes. We shall develop this model further in the next chapter and apply it specifically to several determinants of helping in emergency situations.

4 CHARACTERISTICS OF EMERGENCIES AND THE INTERVENTION PROCESS

In the preceding chapter we considered some of the factors which determine whether an individual will respond to a request for help in nonemergency situations and we reported several field studies in which we attempted to measure the likelihood of assistance in various naturalistic settings. In general, we found that individuals were quite willing to help when asked, and that simple situational variations markedly influenced the likelihood of help. If people are so willing to help in nonemergency situations, they should be even more willing to help in emergencies, in which the need for help is so much greater. Or should they? Emergencies differ in many ways from the sort of nonemergency situations we have dealt with so far, and these differences have important psychological consequences. The very nature of emergencies tells us a good deal about how people will react to them.

Perhaps the most distinctive characteristic of an emergency is that it involves threat of harm or actual harm. Life, well-being, or property are in danger. At worst, an emergency can claim the lives not only of the victims, but of anyone who intervenes. At best, the major result of any intervention is a restoration of the status quo before the emergency, or more normally, a prevention of further damage to an already damaged person or property. Even if an emergency is successfully dealt with, rarely is anybody better off afterwards than before. Consequently, there are few positive rewards for successful action in an emergency.

These high costs and low rewards put pressure on individuals to ignore a potential emergency, to distort their perceptions of it, or to underestimate their responsibility for coping with it.

The second important feature of an emergency is that it is an unusual and rare event. Fortunately, although he may read about them in newspapers or watch fictionalized accounts on television, the average person probably will encounter few real emergencies in his lifetime. Unfortunately, when he does encounter one, he will have had little direct personal experience in handling such a situation. An individual facing an emergency is untrained and unrehearsed.

In addition to being rare, emergencies differ widely one from another, both in cause and in the specific kind of intervention required to cope with them. The one common requirement is action—but the type of action differs from one emergency to another. A fire and a drowning are both emergencies: one requires the addition of water, the other its removal. Each emergency presents a specific problem and each requires a different type of action. Consequently, unlike other rare events, there is no short list of rules for coping with emergencies. Our culture provides us with little secondhand wisdom about how to deal with them. An individual may cope with the rare event of a formal dinner party by assuming a manner gleaned from late night Fred Astaire movies or from Emily Post, but the stereotypes that the late movies provide for dealing with emergencies are much less accurate. "Charge!" "Women and children first!" "Quick, get lots of hot water and towels!" This is about the extent of the advice offered for dealing with emergencies, and it is singularly inappropriate in most specific real emergency situations.

The fourth basic characteristic of emergencies is that they are unforeseen. They "emerge," suddenly and without warning. Being unexpected, emergencies must be handled without the benefit of forethought and planning, and an individual does not have the opportunity to think through in advance what course of action he should take. He must do his thinking in the immediacy of the situation and has no opportunity to consult others as to the best course of action or to alert others who are especially equipped to deal with emergencies. The individual confronted with an emergency is thrown on his own resources. We have already seen that he does not have much in the way of practiced responses or cultural stereotypes to fall back upon.

Nor does the bystander have much time for consultation or consideration after the emergency begins. A final characteristic of an emergency is that it requires immediate, urgent action. It represents a pressing necessity. If the emergency is not dealt with immediately the situation will deteriorate. The threat will transform itself into damage; the harm will continue or spread. The requirement for immediate action prevents the individual confronted with an emergency from leisurely considering the possible courses of action open to him. It forces him to come to a decision before he has time to consider his alternatives. It places him in a condition of stress.

The picture is a grim one. Faced with a situation in which he can gain no benefit, unable to rely on past experience, on the experience of others, or on forethought and planning, denied the opportunity to consider carefully his course of action, the bystander to an emergency is in an unenviable position. It is perhaps surprising that anyone should intervene at all.

A MODEL OF THE INTERVENTION PROCESS

If an individual is to intervene in an emergency, he must make not just one, but a *series* of decisions. Only one particular set of choices will lead him to take action in the situation. Let us now consider the behavioral and cognitive processes that go on in an individual who is in the vicinity of an emergency. What must he do and decide before he actually intervenes? These decisions and actions may have important implications for predicting whether an individual will act.

Let us suppose that an emergency is actually taking place. A middle aged man walking down the street has a heart attack. He stops short, clutches his chest, and staggers to the nearest building wall, where he slowly slumps to the sidewalk in a sitting position. What determines whether a passerby will come to his assistance?

First, the bystander has to *notice* that something is happening. The external event has to break into his thinking and intrude itself on his conscious mind. He must stop concentrating on his private thoughts or the legs of the pretty girl walking down the street ahead of him and pay attention to this unusual event.

Once the person is aware of the event he must *interpret* it as an emergency. Specifically, he must decide whether this particular event is an emergency or whether it can be explained in more normal ways. It may be that the man slumped on the sidewalk is only an eccentric having a rest or a drunk sleeping it off.

If the bystander concludes that something is indeed wrong, he must next decide that it is his personal *responsibility* to act. Perhaps help is on the way or perhaps someone else might be better qualified to help. Even in a true emergency, it is not clear that everybody present should immediately intrude himself into the situation.

If the person does decide that he should help, he must next consider what *form of assistance* he can give. Should he rush in directly to try to help the victim or should he give his help in a more indirect fashion by calling a doctor or the police?

Finally, of course, he must decide how to *implement* his action. Where is the nearest telephone? Is there a hospital nearby? At this point, the person may finally begin to act in the situation. The socially responsible act is one end point to a *series* of decisions. Only by making the appropriate decision at each of these steps will the bystander intervene.

Noticing something wrong. A person pays only selective attention to his environment. Car horns honk, brakes squeal, steam billows from manholes, and the average city dweller walks on obliviously. As a person continues to live in any environment, he adapts to it and learns to block out certain aspects of it. In so doing he may block out attention to things that signal emergencies. The extent to which he will do so is probably a function of several variables which, interestingly, all seem to be characteristic of urban environments.

It might be predicted, for example, that the noisier an environment, the more necessary it is to block out stimulus input, and the less likely it is that a person will notice an emergency. Likewise, in a dangerous environment, most people are loath to investigate strange shapes in dark places. And in a new or strange environment, individuals are unable to distinguish the exceptional from the routine.

Finally, the constraints on people's behavior when they are in the presence of others may make them less likely to notice an emergency. In a group of strangers it is impolite to pay too much attention to another person or to what he is doing. Chapter 6 describes an experimental result concerning this question.

Deciding the event is an emergency. Once an event is noticed, an onlooker must decide whether or not it is an emergency. Many events are rather ambiguous in this respect. Smoke pouring from a building may be the result of fire—but incinerators and steam presses are often to blame. Screams in the street may indicate an assault—or merely a family quarrel.

To the extent that an emergency is ambiguous, the bystander is free to interpret it in a number of ways. Many things will probably help determine this choice of interpretation, including his past history, his personality, and his present mood, but two things are of special interest—the extent to which the individual is motivated to avoid belief that it is an emergency, and the way he is influenced by the reactions of other bystanders.

We have mentioned earlier that an emergency is a situation in which nobody—whether victim or bystander—has much to gain. If a bystander to a potential emergency can convince himself that nothing really is wrong, he can avoid any conflict about whether to take action. Obviously, there are pressures on him not to believe in the reality of a given emergency and to downgrade its seriousness. In Chapter 9, we shall report an experiment which tests whether such pressures are sufficient to affect belief.

One of the basic facts to emerge from six decades of research in social psychology is that people influence each other—far more, often, than they themselves imagine. People depend on the reactions of others around them to tell them what to believe and how to behave. When faced with a possible emergency, an individual will be considerably influenced by the way in which other people act. If everyone else seems to regard the event as not being serious and the proper course of action as nonintervention, this will strongly affect the individual. He will perceive the situation as less critical and be less likely to act. The consequences of this social influence process prove to be of major importance. In Chapter 5 its theoretical implications will be developed. In Chapters 6, 7, and 8 its importance in determining bystander reactions will be demonstrated.

Deciding on degree of personal responsibility. Even if our observer has noticed an event and identified it as an emergency, this does not automatically mean that *he* will assume responsibility for helping. Several things determine whether the observer will feel a responsibility to handle the situation himself. Among these variables are whether the victim "deserves" help, the competence of the bystander, the relationship between the bystander and the victim, and whether responsibility is shared among a number of bystanders.

Although it may be contrary to our egalitarian ideals, most of us, when faced with the poor, the suffering, and the victimized, do consider the extent to which they deserve, as well as need, our pity, our sympathy, or our help. For example, it seems likely that more hands will be extended to a frail and aged woman sprawled on the sidewalk than to a college sophomore. Such characteristics of the victim as his sex, age, physical condition, socioeconomic class, or race can be expected to markedly influence the extent to which he receives help.

Even when serious harm is being done, the victim may be seen as less deserving if he brought his plight upon himself than if his mishap was accidental. If a bully starts a fight, a bystander might be prompted to intervene. If, however, the bully's victim had pugnaciously announced that he could lick any man in the bar, a bystander might be less likely to help. People who "ask for it" rarely inspire anybody to intervene when they "get it."

Other factors affect the extent to which a particular bystander sees himself as being generally responsible. For example, males in our society are expected to know how to deal with most emergencies; females are not. Such other personal characteristics as age, physical condition, and social role (e.g., police) should also affect the extent to which the bystander feels and is felt to be responsible.

A particular bystander might feel especially responsible for a certain victim when a relationship already exists between them. Obviously, a man is more likely to attempt to rescue his wife than he is to save a stranger. Less obviously, he may be led to help a mere acquaintance, even if there is no friendship involved.

A final and very important factor involved in determining the amount of responsibility felt by any one bystander is the number of other people he thinks are present and available to help. When only one bystander is present at an emergency situation, if help is to be given it must be he who gives it. The situation is not so clear when a crowd of bystanders are present. Then the responsibility for intervention is diffused among the bystanders and focuses on no single one. In these circumstances, each person may feel less responsibility to help the victim. "Why me?" he can say. Chapter 10 will develop this idea and Chapter 11 will summarize several experiments dealing with these variables.

Deciding the specific mode of intervention. Once a person notices an event and decides that it is an emergency and that he personally is responsible for coping with it, it is still necessary for him to decide *how* to deal with it. What specific action should he take? Two general alternatives seem possible. The first is the set of behaviors that might be described as "direct intervention"—stepping in to break up a fight, or grabbing an extinguisher to put out a fire. These acts are the most visible, direct, and obvious ones to take.

Less directly, there are also a set of acts that can be called "detour interventions." One might call the police to stop a fight or the firemen a fire. In general, detour interventions consist of reporting the emergency to the relevant authority rather than attempting to cope with it directly.

Both direct and detour interventions have their advantages and difficulties. On the one hand, since direct intervention is the most obvious thing to do, little ingenuity is required to think of it. However, direct intervention often will require considerable skill. For instance, if someone is being shocked by an electric appliance, a woman might not have the know-how to remove a fuse before grabbing hold of the victim. She may not have the strength to do so, or the risks to herself may be so great that she does not even make the attempt. In general, the kind of direct intervention necessary in an emergency often is obvious, but the required action may be too difficult or dangerous to perform.

The problems involved with successful detour intervention are rather different; the action that one ought to take may not immediately come to mind simply because it is circuitous rather than straightforward. A person faced with a possible emergency may be neither calm nor clear, and he may not be able to figure out the appropriate detour behavior. Once the possibility of the detour is decided on, however, it usually does not require a great deal of skill, strength, or courage to carry it out—usually a telephone call is all that is necessary.

Implementing the intervention. If a bystander has passed through each of the preceding choice points and has decided how to intervene, all that remains is the actual act. Typically, once an individual decides to help, he will have little difficulty in implementing his decision. If the required actions are complicated or difficult, however, he may have trouble, for the stress and urgency generated by the emergency may interfere with his motor performance and make even a moderately difficult task seem quite hard. In a dramatic and controversial series of experiments, Berkun, Bialek, Kern, and Yagi * have provided a good demonstration of these difficulties.

In one of their experiments, they assigned soldiers to a small shack

* Berkun, M. M., Bialek, H. M., Kern, R. P. and Yagi, K. Experimental studies of psychological stress in man. *Psychological Monographs,* 1962, 76, 1–39 (Whole No. 534).

overlooking an isolated canyon to set up a remote control circuit for a group of men wiring in some explosives in the canyon below. While they were working, they heard an explosion in the canyon. Then a voice came over the intercom: "Upstairs, can you hear me? Listen, if you can hear me, we had an explosion down here and . . . we got trouble, bad trouble. Man's been hurt, hurt bad. We don't know exactly how bad. Get on the phone. Listen, get on the phone and call Fort Ord. Just ring the operator." But the phone would not work. Although all men tried their best to fix the phone following a complicated series of instructions, soldiers working under these stressful circumstances were much more clumsy and inept in their work than subjects fixing the phone who were merely told that they were being given a test of their ability.

In sum, then, a bystander confronted with an emergency is faced with a series of decisions which he must make under threat, urgency, and stress. The overall decision of whether to intervene or not depends on his choices all along the line—that is, whether he notices an event or not, perceives it as an emergency or not, feels personal responsibility or not, is able to think of the kinds of intervention necessary or not, and has sufficient skill to intervene or not.

5 SOCIAL DETERMINANTS OF BYSTANDER INTERVENTION I: THE SOCIAL INFLUENCE PROCESS

We have seen thus far that the popular tendency to attribute bystander inaction to apathy, indifference, or alienation from social norms does not really explain very much. On the other hand, a better understanding of the failure of bystanders to intervene is possible if we consider the intervention process itself, and those characteristics of emergencies which make it difficult to intervene. Let us now examine specific factors that are involved in the intervention process and that offer a meaningful way to answer the question: Why do bystanders intervene under some circumstances and not under others?

In the widespread publicity that has been given to "apathy" cases, newspapers have emphasized the *number* of bystanders who have watched apathetically. "Thirty-eight Witnesses Watch Victim Die," read the headlines. "Eleven Do Nothing as Man is Stabbed." In part, this emphasis on numbers is due to the sheer magnitude of apathy demonstrated. If one or two people failed to intervene, we might be able to understand their inaction. But when 38, or 11, or hundreds of people stand and watch, we are shocked and frightened.

The fact that so many people have watched an emergency and done nothing is disturbing because it is surprising. Ordinarily we would expect that the more people who witness an emergency, the more likely it might be that someone would act. This should be especially true in situations where the risk of intervention may be too great for any one individual to shoulder. Further, if externally enforced norms were important determinants of behavior, we should again expect that individual bystanders would be more likely to act if they were in public than if they were alone. In public, others can see their inaction and comment negatively on it. Alone, they can leave the scene of the emergency and no one will be the wiser. The Provo in the *New Yorker* cartoon might have been more likely to stick his finger in the dike if other people were in sight and able to see him. He might have been more likely to intervene if others were present and able to help him. At least, that is the popular impression.

The *number* of people who stand and watch is what shocks us; it also may be a key to their behavior. For, while the number of people present at an emergency does determine to a very important degree what they will do, it does so in a way opposite to that usually assumed. Although it seems obvious that the more people who watch an emergency, the more likely it is that someone will help, what really happens is exactly the reverse. *The presence of other people serves to inhibit the impulse to help.* If each member of a group of bystanders is aware that other people are also present, each will be less likely to notice the emergency, less likely to decide that it is an emergency, and less likely to act even if he thinks there is an emergency. These effects are due to the fact that each person can both see and be seen by the others.

EFFECTS OF BEING SEEN BY OTHERS

In a crowd of people, each person knows that others are watching his appearance, his reactions, and his behavior. A person in public will feel ashamed and embarrassed if he violates rules of public behavior. He will forebear picking his nose or scratching himself, preferring to suffer discomfort rather than be seen behaving in an unseemly manner.

The rules of public behavior may constrain a person's behavior in several ways that make it less likely that he will intervene in an emergency. Americans consider it bad manners to look too closely at other people in public. We are taught to have a decent respect for the privacy of others, and when surrounded by strangers, express this respect by closing our ears to their conversation and by not staring at them—we are embarrassed if caught doing otherwise. The fact that everybody in a crowd is on his best public behavior—staring off into space or down at the ground—however, may prevent anybody from

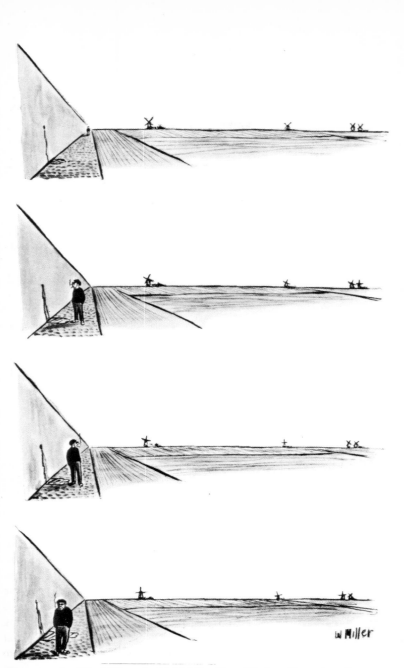

Drawing by W. Miller; © 1966 The New Yorker Magazine, Inc.

noticing the first subtle signs of an emergency. It may delay the realization that something strange is happening, perhaps to the point where it is no longer possible to intervene easily.

Once a person has noticed an emergency, the presence of other people may inhibit his response to it. Before a person sees an emergency, he may be immersed in his daily routine. Faced with an emergency, he is faced with a choice for which he did not ask—whether to intervene or not. Not intervening does not mean doing nothing; it means going on with the well-practiced routine of life. Intervention may require that the person take complicated and nonroutine actions, and that he take them in public.

To cope with an emergency, a dignified Wall Streeter may have to run for the police, or a high-school girl give artificial respiration. A person may be afraid that he will perform these complicated or undignified tasks rather badly and thus lose face in public. As the word perform suggests, the bystander to an emergency is offered the chance to step up on stage, a chance that should be every actor's dream. But in this case, it is every actor's nightmare. He hasn't rehearsed the part very well and he must play it when the curtain is already up. The greater the number of other people present, the more possibility there is of losing face.

The presence of other people may thus inhibit action—and it may also prevent each bystander from even showing his concern. Americans consider it desirable to appear poised and collected in time of stress—to play it or keep it cool. The studied nonchalance of patients in a dentist's waiting room, for instance, bears no relation to the pain they are sure is awaiting them. No member of a crowd wants to be the first to fly off the handle, the one to cry "Wolf!" when no wolf may really be present. Too great a show of concern may in itself be embarrassing, and it also may prematurely commit the bystander to a course of action he has not had a chance to think through. Until he decides what to do, each member of a crowd, however truly concerned and upset he may be about the plight of a victim, may try to maintain a calm demeanor, an unruffled front.

THE EFFECTS OF SEEING OTHERS

A bystander in a crowd is aware that the others can see him and judge his actions, but he is also able to see the others and observe their reactions to the potential emergency. Faced with an ambiguous situation, uncertain what to believe or what to do, he is likely to look to others for guidance as to how he should behave, just as a socially insecure individual at a formal dinner party looks at others to find out which fork to use.

This may sound like slavish conformity, but it would be unwise to condemn it too harshly. Ordinarily we derive much valuable information about new situations from how others around us behave. The habit of looking through more than one pair of eyes enhances our perception. It is a rare and probably unintelligent traveller who, in picking a roadside restaurant, chooses to stop at one with no other cars in the parking lot. If he does, his wife, his stomach, or his pocketbook will explain its unpopularity. It is ordinarily intelligent to consider how other people interpret an event before deciding upon one's own interpretation.

The interpretations that others are making may be discovered by discussing the situation, but they may also be inferred from facial expressions and behavior. A whistling man with his hands in his pockets obviously does not believe that he is in the midst of a crisis. A passive bystander who does not respond to a room filling with smoke obviously does not attribute it to fire. Another's reactions may be as useful as his words in telling us how he interprets a situation and what he thinks is appropriate behavior under the circumstances.

Occasionally the reactions of others provide false information as to the true state of their feelings—and this may be especially likely in a potential emergency. If each member of a group is trying to appear calm and not overreact to the possibility of danger, each other member, in looking to him for guidance, may be misled into thinking that he is not concerned. Looking at the *apparent* impassivity and lack of reaction of the others, each individual is led to believe that nothing really is wrong. Each may be led (or misled) by the others to define the situation as less critical than he would if alone. Until someone acts, each person sees only other nonresponding bystanders, and is likely to be influenced not to act himself. A state of "pluralistic ignorance" may develop in which each person decides that since nobody is concerned, nothing is wrong. Meanwhile, the danger may be mounting to the point where a single individual, uninfluenced by the seeming calm of others, would react.

In strange or unfamiliar circumstances, individuals may be more than usually influenced by the reactions of those around them. If he is uncertain about whether the circumstance represents an emergency, the stress and fear generated by this uncertainty may hamper the individual's capacity to think for himself and make him especially susceptible to social influence. In an experiment designed to demonstrate the point that stress can lead to increased susceptibility to influence, Darley * warned some subjects that they would later receive a series of powerful electric shocks and informed others that they would not. He then gave all subjects a hearing test in which they heard a number of clicks and were asked to tell how many clicks they had heard. Since a number of subjects were tested at the same time, each subject heard the estimates made by the others. Several times during the hearing tests, it was arranged that the estimates each subject heard were incorrect. Frightened subjects under the stress of anticipated electric shock were more likely to conform to the incorrect majority in their own estimates than were nonfrightened subjects.

Although bystander inaction is popularly thought to be a sign of apathy or alienation, we suspect that other explanations may be more appropriate. In general, we suggest, factors affecting the process by which an individual interprets an emergency may be more important determinants of his action than his general motivation to help others. Specifically, we think that the number of other people present at an emergency may have important effects on whether any individual will intervene.

In public, people tend to feel constrained from expressing too much emotion or from making fools of themselves. These constraints may themselves tend to inhibit action by individuals in a group, but in conjunction with the processes of social influence, they may be expected to have especially powerful effects. As each person in an ambiguous and potentially dangerous situation looks to others to gauge their reactions, each may be falsely led to believe that the others are not concerned, and consequently to be less concerned himself. This state of pluralistic ignorance may make each member of a group less likely to act than he would have been had he witnessed the emergency alone.

The experiments reported in the next three chapters provide evidence for the idea that the presence of other people may prevent an individual from intervening in an emergency.

* Darley, J. M. Fear and social comparison as determinants of conformity behavior. *Journal of Personality and Social Psychology,* 1966, *4,* 73–78.

6 WHERE THERE'S SMOKE...

The process a person must go through if he is to intervene in an emergency requires first that the individual notice the event; second, that he define the situation as an emergency; third, that he decide that he himself is responsible for taking action; and finally, that he choose a particular course of action to take. At each stage of the process, it is possible for an individual to make a definition or decision that effectively removes him as a potential helping agent, and there are a number of variables which may influence the likelihood of his deciding not to intervene. The number of other people actually at or imagined to be present at the scene of an emergency is one of the most critical of such variables, since there are a variety of ways in which the presence of additional bystanders may inhibit the urge to help.

However reasonable these ideas may seem in the abstract, they require empirical verification before we can have much confidence in them. Although the model is consistent with reports given by bystanders at a number of emergencies, not all the conclusions to which it leads are self-evident. In this chapter and the ones to follow we shall describe experiments designed to provide empirical support for the model and to test its major predictions.

Virtually the only way to study how people react to emergencies is actually to observe them in such situations. As we shall show below, people tend to be relatively unrealistic when they try to imagine how they would respond in an emergency. For the most part, they are sure *they* would have helped—even though they read in the newspapers that others had not. To ourselves we tend to be heroes, and even if we have doubts, we are not likely to admit them to psychologists. In this area in particular, actions really do speak louder than words.

Unfortunately for sociological research, if not our private lives, emergencies are rare events; they occur infrequently and unpredictably. We could stalk real-life emergencies like big game hunters, but we would observe them only rarely. Even if we bagged one, chances are it would not help us much—emergencies are also unique. In order to pinpoint causal factors operating in emergencies, it is necessary to look at the reactions of people in many situations which differ only in specifiable ways. Ambulance chasing, besides being unsavory, would be scientifically unprofitable.

So, with a good deal of trepidation, we decided to create our own emergencies, attempting to simulate them as realistically as possible in a situation in which it is possible to *repeat* the emergency for each of a number of individuals and to *control* important features of the situation. Within such a relatively constant and controllable framework, specific conditions can be experimentally varied in order to test their effects. Since the emergency, although (hopefully) real to the subjects, was under control, we were able to observe the amount of stress it put on the subjects, and to terminate it if the stress seemed too great.

In order to provide as broad a basis as possible for the model of bystander action, we constructed a number of different types of emergencies. Real-life emergencies vary along an enormous number of dimensions: they may involve danger to life, to health, or to property. They may involve danger to one person, to several persons, or to the bystander himself. They may result from accident, from viciousness, from human error, or from act of God. The experiments reported below were designed to study the responses of individuals who found smoke pouring into their room, heard a bully beating up a child, listened to a young lady have a serious accident, saw a thief stealing money or a case of beer, or thought someone was undergoing a severe epileptic seizure.

EXPERIMENT 6.   WHERE THERE'S SMOKE, THERE'S (SOMETIMES) FIRE *

In this first experiment, we wanted to create an ambiguous but potentially dangerous situation, expose each of a number of people to this situation alone or together, and observe their reactions—whether or

* This experiment is reported more fully in Latané, B. & Darley, J. M. Group inhibition of bystander intervention. *Journal of Personality and Social Psychology*, 1968, *10*, 215–221. We thank Keith Gerritz and Lee Ross who assisted in running the study.

not they tried to intervene. We chose to use a room filling up with smoke, expecting that subjects who interpreted the smoke as fire would act promptly—in order to save their own skins, if not those of other people in the building. Subjects who interpreted the smoke as something else than fire should be less apt to act.

We presented the emergency to individuals either alone, in the presence of two passive others (confederates of the experimenter who were instructed to notice the emergency but remain indifferent to it), or in groups of three. It was our expectation that individuals faced with the passive reactions of the confederates would be influenced by them and thus less likely to take action than single subjects. We also predicted that the constraints on behavior in public combined with the processes of social influence would lessen the likelihood that members of three-person groups would act to cope with the emergency.

PROCEDURE

Our subjects were male Columbia University students living on or near campus. After picking a student's name from a registration list, we telephoned him and invited him to take part in an interview about problems of urban life. We told him that we were interested in interviewing a number of people about their reactions to living in large metropolitan areas, that we were concentrating on Columbia University students because they were intelligent and articulate, and that we had picked his name at random from the student directory. He was offered no reward except the satisfaction of cooperating in a large-scale study and the opportunity to express his views. Probably for the latter reason, almost all of the students we contacted volunteered to take part.

Once he had agreed to take part in the interview, a specific appointment was set up and the student was given directions about being interviewed. He was told to appear at a waiting room in one of the university buildings where he would find some preliminary forms to work on while he awaited being called for the interview. Since he found the waiting room on his own, the subject had no contact, other than the telephone call, with the experimenters while the experiment was in progress.

At the appointed time, the subject came by himself to a medium-sized waiting room equipped with several chairs and tables. On the wall was a large sign which informed him that he had come to the proper place, requested him to sit and wait for the interviewer, and instructed him to fill out one of the preliminary forms stacked in the corner. The subject usually looked briefly around the room, picked up one of the forms, sat at the table, and began to work.

The emergency. After he had worked on the questionnaire for several minutes, we began to introduce smoke into the waiting room through a small vent in the wall. The smoke was chemical, formed by the reaction of titanium tetrachloride and water vapor (the same technique used to produce the billboard smoke rings in Times Square). It consisted of a suspension of titanium dioxide in air, creating a moderately fine-textured, clearly visible stream of white smoke. For the entire experimental period, or until the subject took action, the smoke continued to flow into the room in irregular puffs. By the end of four minutes, enough smoke had filtered into the room to obscure vision, produce a mildly acrid odor, and interfere with breathing.

RESULTS

The typical subject, when alone, behaved in a very reasonable manner. Usually, shortly after the smoke began to jet into the room, the subject would glance up from his questionnaire and notice the smoke (perhaps from the corner of his eye). He would show a slight but noticeable startle reaction and then undergo a brief period of indecision, perhaps returning briefly to his questionnaire, before again staring at the smoke. Soon, most subjects would get up from their chairs, walk over to the vent, and investigate it closely, sniffing the smoke, waving their hands in it, and feeling for temperature changes. Gaining little enlightenment from this investigation, the usual subject would show several more signs of hesitation, but finally walk out of the room. Finding somebody in the hall who looked as if he belonged there, he would calmly report to him the presence of the smoke. No subject showed any signs of panic. Most simply said, "There's something strange going on in there: there seems to be some sort of smoke coming through the wall . . ." Once the subject had reported the smoke, he was told that the situation would be taken care of and he was shown to another room. Soon one of us arrived to discuss the true nature of the experiment with him.

That was the typical response. Half the subjects reported the smoke to someone within two minutes of first having noticed it. Three-quarters of the 24 people who were in this condition reported the smoke within four minutes of its introduction. Six individuals in this condition, however, failed to report the smoke. They stayed in the waiting room as it filled up with smoke, doggedly working on their questionnaires. After six minutes, partly out of compassion, but partly from the conviction that if they had not yet responded, they never would, the experimenter came to the door and told them it was time for the interview.

That then is how subjects who were alone in the waiting room acted: for the most part very reasonably and responsibly. Even under the ambiguous conditions of artificial smoke, 75 percent of these subjects responded effectively to the situation. Although not thrown into a state of panic, most subjects decided that the situation was dangerous enough to warrant reporting. Let us turn now to the behavior of subjects in the second condition, identical to this one in all respects except one—the presence of other people.

Two passive confederates. In this condition, subjects were recruited in the same way as in the Alone condition, and were treated identically with one exception: two other persons waited with them for the interview. Although the subject did not realize it, these other two persons were actually confederates of the experimenter, and throughout the time they sat in the waiting room, they behaved in a fashion that had been rehearsed in advance. Sometimes both were in the room when the naive subject arrived, sometimes both arrived after he did, and sometimes one arrived before and one after the subject. As soon as they entered the room, they took chairs and began to fill out the preliminary form; when the smoke appeared the stooges were instructed to look up, notice the smoke, stare at it briefly, shrug their shoulders, and return to their questionnaires, continuing to work. They made no attempt to communicate with the subject, and if the subject spoke to them, they replied briefly and noncommittally. "I dunno," they muttered, and continued to fill out their questionnaires, waving away smoke to do so.

The confederates were young males who looked and dressed like Columbia undergraduates. To make sure that whatever results emerged from this condition were not due to idiosyncratic attributes of the confederates, we drew different pairs of confederates from twelve persons who were available to take part.

The behavior of subjects run with two passive confederates was dramatically different from that of subjects in the Alone condition. As compared to the response rate of 75 percent in the Alone condition, only one of the ten subjects run in the two Passive Confederates condition reported the smoke. The other nine subjects stayed in the waiting room for the full six minutes while it continued to fill up with smoke, doggedly working on their questionnaires and waving the fumes away from their faces. They coughed, rubbed their eyes, and opened the window—but they did not report the smoke. The difference between the Alone condition and the Two Passive Confederates condition is highly significant ($p < .002$).

TABLE 8
Frequency of Reporting in the Alone and Two Passive Confederates Conditions

Condition	N	Reporters	Nonreporters
Alone	24	18	6
Two passive confederates	10	1	9

Three naive bystanders condition. In the final condition of this experiment, three naive subjects were tested together. In general these subjects did not know each other, although in two groups subjects reported a nodding acquaintanceship with another subject. Since subjects arrived at slightly different times and since they each had individual questionnaires to work on, they did not introduce themselves to each other, or attempt anything but the most rudimentary conversation.

Because there were three subjects present and available to report the smoke in the Three Naive Bystanders condition as compared to only one subject at a time in the Alone condition, a simple comparison between the two conditions is not appropriate. On the one hand, we cannot compare speeds in the Alone condition with the average speed of the three subjects in a group, since, once one subject in a group had reported the smoke, the pressures on the other two disappeared. They legitimately could (and did) feel that the emergency had been handled, and that any action on their part would be redundant and potentially confusing. Therefore, we used the speed of the *first* subject in a group to report the smoke as our dependent variable. However, since there were three times as many people available to respond in this condition as in the Alone condition, we would expect an increased likelihood that *at least* one person would report the smoke even if the subjects had no influence whatsoever on each other. Therefore, we mathematically created "groups" of three scores from the Alone condition to serve as a base line.

In contrast to the complexity of this procedure, the results were quite simple. Subjects in the Three Naive Bystanders condition were markedly inhibited from reporting the smoke. Since 75 percent of the Alone subjects reported the smoke, we would expect over 98 percent of the three-person groups to include at least one reporter.* In fact, in only 38 percent of the eight groups in this condition did even one person report the smoke ($p < .001$). Of the 24 people run in these eight groups, only one person reported the smoke within the first four minutes before the room got noticeably unpleasant. Only three people reported the smoke within the entire experimental period.

Cumulative distribution of report times. Figure 1 presents the cumulative frequency distributions of report times for all three conditions. The figure shows the proportion of subjects in each condition who had reported the smoke by any point in time following the introduction of the smoke. For example, 55 percent of the subjects in the Alone condition had reported the smoke within two minutes, but the smoke had been reported in only 12 percent of the three-person groups by that time. After four minutes, 75 percent of the subjects in the Alone condition had reported the smoke; no additional subjects in the group condition had done so. The curve in Figure 1 labelled "hypothetical three-person groups" is based upon scores obtained from subjects in the Alone condition. It is the expected report times for groups in the three-person condition if the members of the groups had no influence whatever upon each other.

It can be seen in Figure 1 that for every point in time following the introduction of the smoke, a considerably higher proportion of subjects in the Alone condition had reported the smoke than had subjects in either the Two Passive Confederates condition or in the Three Naive Subjects condition. The curve for the third condition, although considerably below the Alone curve, is even more substantially inhibited with respect to its proper comparison, the curve of hypothetical three-person groups. These differences are all strongly significant ($p < .01$).

One final point deserves mention: it appears superficially that there

* The expected proportion of groups in which at least one person will have acted by a given time is $1 - (1 - p)^n$ where p is the proportion of single individuals who act by that time and n is the number of persons in the group.

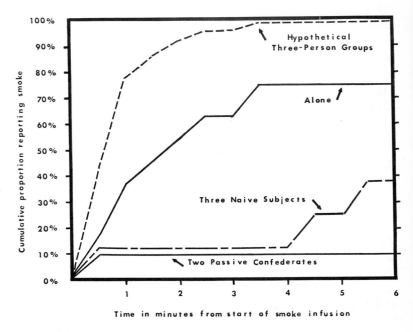

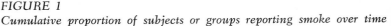

FIGURE 1

Cumulative proportion of subjects or groups reporting smoke over time

is a somewhat higher likelihood of response from groups of three naive subjects than from subjects in the Two Passive Confederates condition. However, again, this comparison is not justified: there are three people free to act in one condition instead of just one. If we mathematically combine scores for subjects in the Two Passive Confederates condition in a similar manner to that described above for the Alone condition, we obtain an expected likelihood of response of .27 as the hypothetical baseline. This is not significantly different from the .37 obtained in the actual three-subject groups.

Noticing the smoke. In observing a subject's reactions to the introduction of smoke, careful note was taken of the exact moment when he first saw the smoke (all report latencies were computed from this time). This was a relatively easy observation to make, for the subjects invariably showed a distinct, if slight, startle reaction. The frequencies with which the smoke was noticed within the first five seconds after its introduction for subjects in the Alone and combined Together groups are shown in Table 9. The presence of other persons delayed, slightly but very significantly, the noticing of the smoke ($p < .01$).

TABLE 9
Frequency of Noticing Smoke within Five Seconds

Condition	Notice	Not Notice	Percent Noticing
Alone	15	9	63
Combined together	11	32 *	26

* Does not include 9 subjects told of smoke by their partners.

The median latency of noticing the smoke was under five seconds in the Alone condition; the median time at which the first (or only) subject in each of the combined Together conditions noticed the smoke was 20 seconds. This difference does not account for group-induced inhibition of reporting since the report latencies were computed from the time the smoke was first noticed.

This finding can be explained in terms of the previous suggestions concerning the behavior people feel that it is appropriate to exhibit in public places. Unlike solitary subjects, who often glanced idly about the room while filling out their questionnaires, subjects in groups usually kept their eyes closely fixed on their own questionnaires, probably to avoid appearing rudely inquisitive.

Postexperimental interview. After six minutes, whether or not the subjects had reported the smoke, the interviewer looked into the waiting room and asked the subject to come with him to the interview. After seating the subject in his office, the interviewer made some general apologies about keeping the subject waiting for so long, hoped the subject had not become too bored and asked if he "had experienced any difficulty while filling out the questionnaire." At this point most subjects mentioned the smoke. The interviewer expressed mild surprise and asked the subject to tell him what had happened. Thus each subject gave an account of what had gone through his mind during the smoke infusion.

Subjects who had reported the smoke were relatively consistent in later describing their reactions to it. They thought the smoke looked somewhat "strange," they were not sure exactly what it was or whether it was dangerous, but they felt it was unusual enough to justify some examination. "I wasn't sure whether it was a fire but it looked like something was wrong." "I thought it might be steam, but it seemed like a good idea to check it out."

Subjects who had not reported the smoke also were unsure about exactly what it was, but they uniformly said that they had rejected the idea that it was a fire. Instead, they hit upon an astonishing variety of alternative explanations, all sharing the common characteristic of interpreting the smoke as a nondangerous event. Many thought the smoke was either steam or air-conditioning vapors, several thought it was smog, purposely introduced to simulate an urban environment, and two (from different groups) actually suggested that the smoke was a "truth gas" filtered into the room to induce them to answer the questionnaire accurately (surprisingly, they were not disturbed by this conviction). Predictably, some decided that "it must be some sort of experiment" and stoically endured the discomfort of the room rather than overreact.

Despite the obvious and powerful report-inhibiting effect of other bystanders, subjects almost invariably claimed that they had paid little or no attention to the reactions of the other people in the room. Although the presence of other people actually had a strong and pervasive effect on the subjects' reactions, they were either unaware of this or unwilling to admit it.

DISCUSSION

As predicted, most subjects who faced the smoke alone reacted to it; most subjects who faced it in groups did not react. Single subjects, although not convinced that they were confronted with a serious fire, and certainly not in a state of panic, nevertheless thought the situation serious enough to report to an authority. Subjects in groups were led by the apparent indifference of each other to decide that the smoke did not represent dangerous fire, and that the proper course of action was to stay right where they were.

The presence of other people is not always so successful in inhibiting the response to smoke. We have all heard of horrible panics, where crowds of smoke-crazed people stampede for an exit, killing more people by their actions than were endangered by the fire itself. In Chicago's

Iroquois Theater in 1903, for example, the appearance of smoke started a panicked rush for the exits. Eddie Foy, who was onstage at the time, describes the aftermath of the event:

> But it was only inside the house that the greatest loss of life occurred, especially on the stairways leading down from the second balcony. Here most of the dead were trampled or smothered, though many jumped or fell over the balustrade to the floor of the foyer. In places on the stairways, particularly where a turn caused a jam, bodies were piled seven or eight feet deep. Firemen and police confronted a sickening task in disentangling them. An occasional living person was found in the heaps, but most of these were terribly injured. The heel prints on the dead faces mutely testified to the cruel fact that human animals stricken by terror are as mad and ruthless as stampeding cattle. Many bodies had the clothes torn from them, and some had the flesh trodden from their bones.
>
> Never elsewhere had a great fire disaster occurred so quickly. From the start of the fire until all in the audience either escaped, died, or lay maimed in the halls and alleys, took just eight minutes. In that eight minutes more than 500 perished.

In our experiment the presence of other people inhibited the response to smoke; in the Iroquois Theater, it exacerbated it. What makes the difference?

Panics do not inevitably occur whenever some one smells smoke in a theater or nightclub. Educated audiences may tend to resist panic; quick-thinking actors and band leaders may act to prevent panic. The purposeful rendition of our National Anthem has been credited with keeping many panic-ripe situations from turning into disasters. In fact, it is possible that the presence of an audience, at least in the early stages of a theater fire, tends, as in our smoke experiment, to make people stay in their seats. They may brood on the possibility of fire, they may become more and more uneasy, but, until someone breaks for an exit, they are likely to remain where they are.

The presence of really large numbers of people does create a situation that is different from our smoke-filled room. The presence of several thousand people increases the chance that at least one will act impulsively. As Eddie Foy observed: "Somebody had of course yelled 'Fire!' There is almost always a fool of that species in an audience; and there are always hundreds of people who go crazy the minute they hear the word." One person may act impulsively, and by the visibility and drama of his action, destroy the apparent unanimity of unconcern, the state of pluralistic ignorance, and encourage other members of the crowd to express their previously hidden fear and concern.

The presence of large numbers of people, given a limited number of exits, may also lead people to believe that not everybody can be saved. Having read about panics, an individual may come to fear the possibility that others may panic as much as he fears the possibility of fire itself. He may head for the exits, not to escape the fire, but to escape the other members of the audience. To avoid the consequences of panic, such a person may do his share in starting one.

7 THE BYSTANDER AND THE VICTIM

In the experiment with the smoke-filled room it was demonstrated that male college students, when faced with the ambiguous but potentially dangerous sight of smoke filtering into a small room, are less likely to take action when there are two other male college students present than when they are alone. We would, of course, like to think that it demonstrates more than this—indeed that it shows that *in general*, an individual's response to emergencies can be inhibited by the presence of others.

Usually, if a scientist has predicted a relationship, and his prediction is upheld in the one out of all possible situations in which he happens to test the relationship, he will argue that there is no reason to believe it would not also work in any other situation in which he might have tested it. He is usually justified in assuming generality, at least until evidence appears to the contrary. In the present case, however, there are a number of features of the smoke-filled room which may distinguish it from other types of emergencies and thus limit the generality of the results.

For example, the smoke we employed provided an ambiguous stimulus—possibly dangerous, possibly not. Smoke is an indication of fire, but it is also similar to air-conditioner vapors, steam from a heating system, or the by-product of cigars and cigarettes. It is possible that the influence of other people is limited to those situations in which such ambiguity exists. Also, the smoke represented a danger to the subject himself as much as to other people in the building. Perhaps the presence of other people merely led to some misguided sense of bravery in which the subject resisted action in order to show that he was not panicked by the smoke.

Aside from the lack of generality potentially imposed by the specifics of the experiment, there are also questions about the kinds of other people present. Does the inhibitory effect of other people depend on the fact that in a three-person group, the subject is in a minority? What would happen if only one other person were present? Does the effect depend on the fact that the other people were strangers to the subject? What would happen if the subject were tested with a close friend?

In order to answer these questions, we designed a second experiment, conceptually similar to the smoke study, but specifically different in a variety of details. Rather than using smoke again, we manufactured a new emergency—one that we hoped would be as unambiguous as possible. To avoid the question of personal bravery, we created a situation in which only one person, not the subject himself, was in danger. And to resolve the question of type and number of other people necessary to produce inhibition, we tested subjects in one of four conditions: alone, with *one* passive confederate, with another naive subject, or with a close friend.

Before going into the procedure and results of this second experiment, let us pause briefly to consider what we might expect to find out from it. First, it is clear from the general considerations of Chapter 5 that the inhibitory effects of the presence of other people should not be specific to the smoke situation—we should find the same pattern of results even in very different situations. However, with respect to the question of the effects of friendship, new predictions can be made. Consider the explanations given for the inhibitory effect of other people on the response to emergencies: knowing that others are watching him, the subject may be reluctant to perform any action that might embarrass him, and seeing the others' lack of reaction, the subject may be misled into thinking that the situation is not serious or that action is not appropriate. Both of these explanations lead to the suggestion that friends will be less inhibited than strangers in responding to an emergency. Friends should be less likely to feel embarrassed about acting in front of each other and they should be less likely to misinterpret each other's lack of action.

EXPERIMENT 7. *A LADY IN DISTRESS* *

This experiment employed the same general framework as the smoke-filled room study. Subjects were asked to participate in an irrelevant study, and, while filling out a preliminary questionnaire, they were exposed to an emergency. They were tested alone, with a friend, or with a stranger, and their responses observed.

Since a major point of this study was to determine the effects of prior friendship on dealing with emergencies, we asked subjects in the Two Friends condition to bring a friend with them to the testing session. In order to make this group strictly comparable with subjects in the other conditions, we decided to ask *all* subjects to recruit friends to take part in the experiment. In this way we ensured that subjects in all conditions were equally committed to the experiment, had worked equally hard to take part in it, and were equally able to find a friend willing to take part. Subjects and their friends were scheduled together in the Two Friends condition and at different times in the other conditions.

We telephoned male Columbia undergraduates and asked them, for two dollars, to participate in a survey being conducted by the Consumer Testing Bureau, a market research organization interested in testing the market appeal of a number of adult games and puzzles. Each subject was asked to find a friend who would also be interested in participating. Only subjects who recommended friends, and the friends that they suggested, were used as subjects. Of 156 undergraduates who were contacted, 22 were unable or unwilling to take part, usually due to inability to schedule an appointment. Fourteen subjects who had appointments did not show up on time, leaving a total of 120 subjects who took part in the experiment.

When the subject arrived for his appointment, he was met by an attractive and vivacious young woman who introduced herself as the "market research representative" and showed him to the testing room. This was a small room, separated by a collapsible cloth folding curtain-wall from the "Consumer Testing Bureau Office" next door. The testing room was furnished with a table and several chairs and a number of adult games were scattered about. A large sign giving preliminary

* This study is reported more fully in Latané, B. and Rodin, Judith. A lady in distress: Inhibiting effects of friends and strangers on bystander intervention. *Journal of Experimental Social Psychology*, 1969, 5, 189–202.

instructions covered most of the one-way window in the room. In the office next door, whose door was open, the subject could see a desk, chairs, and a large rather ramshackle bookcase with stacks of paper and equipment arrayed precariously on the top shelf.

The market research representative briefly explained the purposes of the market research survey, and asked the subjects to fill out several preliminary questionnaires containing items dealing with family background and game-playing preferences. While they worked on these preliminary forms, the representative opened the collapsible curtain and said that she would do one or two things next door in her office, but would return in 10 or 15 minutes to show them the games. Each subject thus saw that the curtain was unlocked, easily opened, and that it provided a simple means of entry into the office next door.

The emergency. While they worked on their questionnaires, subjects heard the representative moving around in the next office, shuffling papers, and opening and closing drawers. After about four minutes, if they were listening carefully, they heard her climb up on a chair to get a book from the top shelf. Even if they were not listening carefully, they heard a loud crash and a woman's scream as the chair fell over. "Oh, my God, my foot . . ." cried the representative. "I . . . I . . . can't move . . . it. Oh, my ankle. I . . . can't . . . can't . . . get . . . this thing off . . . me." She moaned and cried for about a minute longer, getting gradually more subdued and controlled. Finally, she muttered something about getting outside, knocked the chair around as she pulled herself up, and limped out, closing the door behind her.

This whole sequence, of course, was prerecorded on high fidelity stereophonic tape, but the subjects next door had no way of knowing that. In fact, only 6 percent of the subjects later reported that they had had even the slightest suspicion that the episode might have been recorded.

The main dependent variable of the study was the type of response made to the emergency and the length of time before that response was made. Subjects could either intervene or not, and if they acted they could do so in several ways. They could go through the curtain and directly assist the victim, they could go out the door and find someone else to help, or most simply, they could just call through the curtain to establish contact with the victim.

If the subject had done none of these things by the end of the tape, the experimenter came limping into the testing room through the door and began an interview, attempting to elicit the subject's reaction to the accident before explaining the true purpose of the experiment. All subjects, of course, received a full explanation of the experiment and a two dollar fee for their participation. Before leaving they were asked to answer a number of questions about their reactions to the experiment and requested not to discuss the experiment with anyone.

Four experimental groups were run. Two provided a replication of the smoke study: subjects were run alone as the only person in the testing room during the course of the emergency or together with a confederate of the experimenter. As in the smoke study, confederates were young males who dressed like college students, but who were instructed to be as passive as possible. If the subject asked any questions or made friendly overtures, they answered with a brief and hopefully neutral gesture or remark, and when they heard the crash next door, they were instructed to look up, stare quizzically at the curtain, shrug their shoulders, and return to work. In order to increase the generality of the results, a number of different confederates were used, but unlike the smoke study, only *one* confederate was present with any given subject.

In a second pair of conditions, two naive subjects were tested together. In half of these pairs, the subjects were strangers to each other; in half they were friends. Subjects in the Two Strangers condition were given their instructions and questionnaires at the same time but were not introduced to each other by the experimenter. (Only one subject in this condition spontaneously introduced himself to the other subject.) Subjects in the Two Friends condition, of course, knew each other quite well: often they were roommates, and several had been childhood friends. Since in the Two Friends and Two Strangers conditions, if one person responded, the situation changed markedly for the other, we counted only the *first* response in a pair.

RESULTS

Mode of intervention. Across all experimental groups, the majority of subjects who intervened did so by pulling back the room divider and coming into the CTB office (61 percent). Few subjects came the roundabout way through the door to offer their assistance (14 percent), and a surprisingly small number (24 percent) chose the easy solution of calling out to offer help. No one tried to find someone else to whom to report the accident. Thus all interveners offered some kind of direct assistance to the injured woman. Since experimental conditions did not differ in the proportions choosing various modes of intervention, the comparisons below will deal only with the total proportions of subjects offering help.

Alone vs. passive confederate conditions. Seventy percent of all subjects who heard the fall while alone in the waiting room offered to help the victim before she left the room. By contrast, the presence of a nonresponsive bystander markedly inhibited helping. Only 7 percent of subjects in the Passive Confederate condition intervened. These subjects seemed upset and confused during the emergency and frequently glanced at the stooge, who continued working on his questionnaire. The difference between the Alone and Passive Confederate conditions is, of course, highly significant (p < .001).

Figure 2 presents the cumulative proportion of subjects who had intervened by any point in time following the accident. For example,

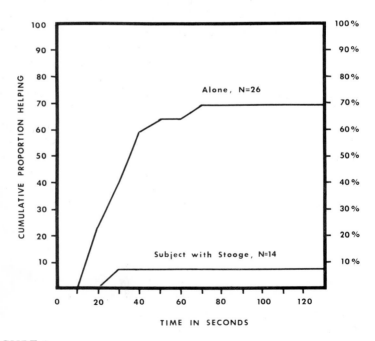

FIGURE 2
Cumulative proportion of subjects helping over time in Alone and Passive Confederate conditions

Figure 2 shows that by the end of 60 seconds, 64 percent of Alone subjects and only 7 percent of subjects tested with a stooge had intervened. The shape of these curves indicates that even had the emergency lasted longer than 130 seconds, little further intervention would have taken place. In fact, over the experiment as a whole, 90 percent of all subjects who ever intervened did so in the first half of the time available to them.

It is clear that the presence of an unresponsive bystander strongly inhibited subjects from offering to help the injured woman. Let us look now at whether this effect depends up some specific characteristic of the passive confederate or upon his unnatural behavior. Will the same social inhibition occur when two naive subjects are tested together?

Alone vs. two strangers conditions. To compare response rates in the Alone and Two Strangers conditions, we again computed a hypothetical base line from the Alone distribution. This base line is graphed in Figure 3, and represents the *expected* cumulative proportion of pairs in which at least one person helps if the members of the pairs are entirely independent (i.e., behave exactly like Alone subjects). Since 70 percent of Alone subjects intervene, we should expect that at least one person in 91 percent of all two-person groups would offer help, if members of a pair had no influence upon each other.

In fact, the results show that members of a pair had a strong influence on each other. In only 40 percent of the groups of subjects in the Two Strangers condition did even one person offer help to the injured woman. Only eight subjects of the 40 who were run in this condition intervened. This response rate is significantly below the hypothetical base rate ($p < .001$). Figure 3 shows that at every point in time, fewer subjects in the Two Strangers condition intervened than would be expected on the basis of the Alone response rate ($p < .01$). This result demonstrates that the presence of another person strongly inhibits individuals from responding, and that this inhibition is not a function of some artificiality of a stooge's behavior.

Stranger vs. passive confederate conditions. The response rate of 40 percent in the Two Strangers condition appears to be somewhat higher than in the 7 percent rate in the Passive Confederate condition. Making a correction similar to that used for the Alone scores, the expected response rate based on the Passive Confederate condition is 13 percent. This is significantly lower than the response rate in the Two Strangers condition ($p < .05$).

The results above strongly replicate the findings of the smoke study.

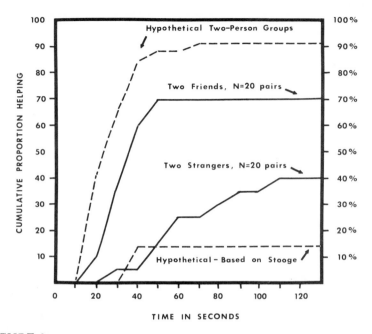

FIGURE 3
Cumulative proportion of pairs of Friends and Strangers helping over time, with hypothetical base lines

In both experiments, subjects were less likely to take action if they were in the presence of passive confederates than if they were alone, and in both studies this effect showed up even when groups of naive subjects were tested together. This congruence of findings from different experimental settings supports their validity and generality; it also helps rule out a variety of explanations suitable to either situation alone. For example, the smoke may have represented a threat to the subject's own personal safety. It is possible that subjects in groups were less likely to respond than single subjects because of a greater concern to appear "brave" in the face of a possible fire. This explanation, however, does not fit the present experiment in which the same pattern of results appeared. In the present experiment, nonintervention cannot signify bravery.

Comparison of the two experiments also suggests that the absolute number of nonresponsive bystanders may not be a critical factor in producing social inhibition of intervention. One passive confederate in the present experiment was as effective as two in the smoke study; pairs of strangers in the present study inhibited each other as much as did trios in the former study.

Let us look now at comparisons involving the condition in which pairs of friends were tested together.

Alone vs. two friends conditions. Pairs of friends often talked about the questionnaire before the accident and sometimes discussed a course of action after the fall. Even so, in only 70 percent of the pairs did even one person intervene. While superficially this appears as high as the Alone condition, again there must be a correction for the fact that two people are free to act. When compared to the 91 percent base rate of hypothetical two-person groups, friends do inhibit each other from intervening (p < .10). Friends were less likely, and they were also slower, to intervene than would be expected on the basis of the Alone rate (p < .05).

Friends vs. strangers conditions. Although pairs of friends were inhibited from helping when compared to the Alone condition, they were significantly faster to intervene than were pairs of strangers (p < .01). The median latency of the first response from pairs of friends was 36 seconds; the median pair of strangers did not respond at all within the arbitrary 130-second duration of the emergency.

How can we account for the differential social inhibition caused by friends and strangers? One sort of explanation which plagues comparisons of friends and strangers in many experiments was ruled out by the present procedure. If some subjects are asked to recruit friends and others are not, different degrees of commitment may be aroused. In this experiment, all subjects either recruited friends or were recruited by them, thus equalizing commitment across conditions.

We suggested in the beginning of this chapter that people may be less likely to fear possible embarrassment in front of friends than before strangers, and that friends are less likely to misinterpret each other's inaction than are strangers. If so, social influence should be less likely to lead friends to decide there is no emergency. There is some evidence consistent with this possibility.

When strangers overheard the emergency, they seemed noticeably concerned but confused. Attempting to interpret what they heard and to decide on a course of action, they often glanced furtively at one another, apparently eager to discover the other's reaction yet unwilling to meet eyes and betray their own concern. Friends, on the other hand, seemed better able to convey their concern nonverbally, and often discussed the incident and arrived at a mutual plan of action. Although these observations are admittedly impressionistic, they are consistent with other data. During the emergency, a record was kept of whether the bystanders engaged in verbal conversation. No attempt was made to code the amount or content of what was said, but it was possible to determine whether there was any talking at all in each pair. Only 29 percent of subjects attempted any conversation with the stooge, while 60 percent of the pairs of strangers engaged in some conversation, mostly desultory and often unrelated to the accident. Although the latter rate seems higher than the former, it really is not, since there are two people free to initiate a conversation rather than just one. Friends, on the other hand, were somewhat more likely to talk than strangers. Eighty-five percent of them did so ($p < .15$). Friends, then, may show less mutual inhibition than strangers because they are less likely to develop a state of pluralistic ignorance.

From the victim's viewpoint. In order to determine whether an individual's likelihood of responding is affected by the presence of other people, we have compared scores in the Two Friends and Two Strangers conditions with a hypothetical base rate computed from the distribution of responses in the Alone condition. By this procedure, we have shown that an individual is less likely to respond when he is with either a friend or a stranger. But what of the victim? Under what conditions was she most likely to get help? For this question the use of hypothetical base lines is not relevant; instead it is necessary to look at the actual response rates. The results show that the victim was no better off if two friends heard her cry for help than if only one person did. And when the bystanders were strangers, social inhibition was so strong that the victim actually got help significantly faster, the fewer people who heard her distress (Alone vs. Two Strangers, $p < .01$). In this instance, she would be foolish indeed to count on safety in numbers.

Postexperimental interview. Although the interview began differently for the interveners and noninterveners, all subjects were encouraged to discuss the accident and their reactions to it in some detail before they were told about the tape and the purpose of the experiment.

Subjects who intervened usually claimed that they did so either because the fall sounded very serious or because they were uncertain what had occurred and felt they should investigate. Many talked about intervention as the "right thing to do" and asserted they would help again in any situation.

Many of the noninterveners also claimed that they were unsure what had happened (59 percent), but had decided it was not too serious (46 percent). A number of subjects reported that they thought other people would or could help (25 percent), and three said they refrained out of concern for the victim—they did not want to embarrass her. Whether to accept these explanations as reasons or rationalizations is moot—they certainly do not explain the differences among conditions. The important thing to note is that noninterveners did not seem to feel that they had behaved callously or immorally. Their behavior was generally consistent with their interpretation of the situation. Subjects almost uniformly claimed that in a "real" emergency, they would be among the first to help the victim.

Interestingly, when subjects were asked whether they had been influenced by the presence or action of their co-worker, they were either unwilling or unable to believe that they had. Subjects in the Passive Confederate condition reported, on the average, that they were "very little" influenced by the stooge; subjects in the Two Strangers condition claimed to have been only "a little bit" influenced by each other; and friends admitted to "moderate" influence. Put another way, only 14 percent, 30 percent, and 70 percent of the subjects in these three conditions admitted to at least a "moderate" degree of influence ($p < .01$). These claims, of course, run directly counter to the experimental results, in which friends were the least inhibited and subjects in the Passive Confederate condition most inhibited by the other's actions.

Reactions to the experiment. After the postexperimental interview, debriefing, and payment of the promised two dollars, subjects were asked to fill out a final questionnaire concerning their mood and their reactions to the experiment. Subjects were convincingly assured that their answers would be entirely anonymous and the experimenter departed. On an adjective check list, 85 percent of the subjects said they were "interested," 77 percent "glad to have taken part," 59 percent "concerned about the problem," 33 percent "surprised," 24 percent "satisfied," 18 percent "relieved," 12 percent "happy," 2 percent "annoyed," 1 percent "angry at myself," and 0 percent "angry at the experimenter," "afraid," or "ashamed." One hundred percent said they would be willing to take part in similar experiments in the future, 99 percent that the deceptions were necessary, and 100 percent that they were justified. On a five-point scale, 96 percent found the experiment either "very interesting" or "interesting," the two extreme points. The only sign of a difference in reaction between interveners and noninterveners was that 47 percent of the former and only 24 percent of the latter checked the most extreme interest ($p < .05$). In general, then, reactions to the experiment were highly positive.

DISCUSSION

The results of this experiment provide confirmation of our original hypotheses, and they do so in a new situation, different in several respects from the smoke situation. Subjects in pairs were less likely to interpret the fall as serious and more likely to decide that it would be inappropriate to intervene than were single subjects. Although subjects gave many different reasons for their actions, several hit upon what we thought was a surprising excuse—they did not want to intervene out of concern for the victim. Impressed by their sincerity, we came to realize that they had a point. The victim to an emergency may not always appreciate intervention.

The victim of an emergency, if his plight is not too serious, may resent the offer of help. It may insult him by impugning his ability to cope with his own problems. It may embarrass him by focusing public attention on him at a time when he does not appear at his best. It may put him in the difficult position of having received help, but being unable to reciprocate. For any of these reasons, he may respond with less than perfect gratitude. Unlike the man in the cartoon, he may spurn the help of any would-be Galahad.

Although the behavior of rats provides a poor guide to the behavior of people, an experiment conducted by Latané and Gerritz provides a nice analogy to the situation above. Interested in animal sociability, they observed white rats in a circular arena where the rats could move about freely. When tested in pairs, rats were quite sociable, spending over 50 percent of their time in direct physical contact, chasing each other about, and seeming to have a fine time. At this point, the investigators put a large alligator clip on the tail of one rat, causing him a good deal of pain and distress. At first, the "bystander" rat showed no change in his interest in the "victim." He was no more or less attracted to him than

"Whether we find my contact lens or not, I want to thank all of you anyway for becoming involved."

Drawing by Shirvanian; © 1968 The New Yorker Magazine, Inc.

before the "accident." Whenever the bystander rats approached the victims, however, they would be attacked. Probably out of frustration and pain, the victims snapped at, shoved, bit, and generally made the hapless bystander unwelcome. Within about 15 minutes, most bystanders learned that it does not always pay to meddle with someone in trouble.

8 THE BYSTANDER AND THE THIEF

When a bystander is faced with the possibility of a fire or confronted with the victim of an apparently serious accident, he is more likely to interpret the situation as an emergency, and consequently to take action, if he is alone than if he is in the presence of other bystanders. Fires and accidents certainly are emergencies, but they differ from the emergencies typically encountered in "apathy" stories. They are caused by impersonal agents and do not involve a villain. It is possible that the social influence processes demonstrated so clearly by the smoke and accident studies do not operate within a picture involving a villain such as a rapist, thief, or murderer.

A villain represents a danger not only to the victim, but to anybody who is rash enough to interfere with him. A single individual may be reluctant to tangle with a villain. If it comes to physical violence, his odds are at best equal. At worst, the villain will be armed and vicious. Undeterred from crime, he may be undeterred from violence as well. Even if the individual bystander can avoid immediate physical contact by reporting the villain to the authorities, he still faces future dangers of retribution, either from the villain himself or from his friends. And he may well find himself subpoenaed to appear in court.

When several bystanders witness a crime, the dangers to any one for intervening are lessened. Together, they may be physically able to overpower the criminal. If one or more of them report the crime, they will be less identifiable than a single person, and thus less likely to suffer retribution. If several are witnesses, the chances of any one being called to testify may be lessened. Under these conditions, even if one person is reluctant to take action, the presence of other people as potential risk-sharing allies might embolden him to intervene. These considerations suggest reasons why groups might be more likely than single individuals to intervene in a crime. However, despite these considerations, social inhibitions provided by the presence of other people may still be sufficient to lead individuals to react more quickly to a crime when they are alone than when they are with others. In this chapter we report two experiments that explore this question.

EXPERIMENT 8.   THE HAND IN THE TILL *

Male undergraduates witnessed a theft while waiting for an interview. In one condition, each subject was the sole witness; in another, two subjects were present. The dependent variable was whether the subjects reported the crime.

PROCEDURE

Columbia College freshmen signed up on a volunteer sheet posted in their dormitories to participate in a one-hour interview for a fee of two dollars. After being contacted by telephone to schedule a time, subjects came for their interviews. They were greeted by an attractive receptionist and led into the waiting room. The waiting room was the same as in previous experiments, except that for this experiment it was equipped with a row of five chairs along one wall and a small desk and chair on the opposite wall.

   Among the subjects who arrived was a short, clean-cut student wearing a conservative sport jacket with an open shirt. Although sounds of distant thunder did *not* appear on the sound track, this "subject" was soon to become a criminal. He was, of course, an accomplice of the experimenter.

   When all the subjects had arrived, the receptionist, sitting at her desk, checked off their names on her schedule sheet and announced that they would be individually interviewed by a team of experts from the Institute for the Study of Human Problems on the reactions of college students to the urban environment of New York City. She

---

* This study was conducted by B. Latané and D. Elman.

apologized that the interviews were running a few minutes behind schedule, and, to save time, paid the subjects in advance. Picking up an envelope from her desk, she pulled out several large bills and some smaller ones to pay the subjects their two dollars. To emphasize the large amount of money in the envelope, she asked if anyone in the room had change for twenty dollars. After paying the subjects, she put the remainder of the money (between thirty and fifty dollars) back in the envelope, returned to her desk and sat down, putting the envelope on the top of the desk. Shortly afterward a buzzer sounded, and she left the room, ostensibly to answer the call.

The theft. Several seconds after the receptionist left the room, the Thief stood up, walked over to the desk, and fumbled with a magazine that had been lying on top of it. Then, clumsily but blatantly, seemingly trying to hide his actions but performing in full view of the other subject(s), he reached into the envelope, took out the cash, stuffed it into his jacket pocket, picked up the magazine, and returned to his seat. At no time did he say a word. If addressed, he either ignored the comment, continuing to leaf through his magazine, or answered with an innocent "I don't know what you are talking about."

About one minute after the theft, the receptionist returned. At this time, the subject(s) had an opportunity to report the crime if he was willing to confront the Thief to do so. After half a minute, the receptionist sent the Thief to his "interview." Now the subjects could report the theft without directly confronting the Thief. We were interested, of course, in what proportion of subjects would responsibly report the theft spontaneously to the receptionist.

If the subject did not report the theft, we were concerned to make sure that he had actually seen it, and followed an elaborate procedure to determine this. If the theft had not been reported within one minute after the Thief left for his interview, the receptionist opened her envelope, noticed that some money was missing, and attempted to elicit a report by questioning the subject(s) about the money. Then she sent the subject(s) to another room with a male interviewer, who began by asking some questions about the subject's background and mentioned that the topic for the interview would be "crime on the streets." Gradually during the course of the interview he raised the question of what had happened in the waiting room and asked the subjects to describe their reactions, again trying to find whether the subject had actually noticed the theft. Finally, he explained the deceptions and purposes of the experiment and used the incident as a starting point for a discussion of some of the conditions of life in modern American cities.

RESULTS

Despite the smallness of the room, the absence of things to look at, and the blatant clumsiness of the theft, many subjects steadfastly claimed throughout the entire interview that they had not noticed the crime. Table 10 presents the number of subjects or pairs who noticed, or professed not to have noticed, the theft.

TABLE 10
Frequency of Noticing Theft

Condition	N	Noticed	Did Not Notice
Alone	25	12	13
Together	16 pairs	12 pairs	4 pairs

Fifty-two percent of subjects in the Alone condition claimed not to have noticed the theft, while 25 percent of the Together pairs said they had not seen it. These apparently different noticing rates are really quite similar when we consider that the expected joint probability of two subjects failing to notice the theft if they do not influence each other is the product of the individual probabilities, that is, 27 percent. Unlike the smoke study, the presence of another subject did not inhibit noticing the theft (or, at least, admitting to have noticed the theft).

The high proportion of subjects in both conditions who professed not to have noticed the crime is surprising in light of the obviousness of the theft and the lack of other things to distract their attention. It is also surprising in the light of observers' reports. Observers, watching the scene through a one-way mirror, were convinced, by the direction of subjects' gazes, by their quickly suppressed startle reactions, and by their too carefully studied expressions of nonchalance, that the majority of subjects actually did see the theft.

We suspect that, in one sense, the claim of many subjects that they had not noticed the theft may be accurate. This is, it is possible that many subjects had not *completed* noticing the event. As we shall discuss more fully in the next chapter, noticing the theft would have put subjects in an avoidance-avoidance conflict such that they were torn between the negative alternatives of risking confrontation with the Thief by acting and risking guilt at not acting. A good way to avoid this conflict was not to see the theft at all. Many subjects may have noticed the beginnings of the theft, and without fully thinking about the implications of what they had seen, unconsciously turned their attention away from what was happening.

Other subjects may have noticed the theft, but, anxious to make their nonintervention consistent with their self or public images, may have clung to a story which, to themselves and to the interviewer, provided a perfect justification for not acting. Some of these subjects may have come to believe their story, while others, of course, may not.

Reporting the theft. The widespread failure to notice an obvious crime is an interesting phenomenon, but it also presents a problem for the interpretation of further results. Since it is difficult to determine which of the nonnoticers were genuine and which were fabricators, let us be conservative and look at the proportion of all subjects, noticers and nonnoticers, who reported the crime. In the Alone condition, 24 percent of all subjects spontaneously reported the theft to the receptionist. From this, we would expect that at least 42 percent of the pairs would include at least one person who would report the theft. Actually, in only 19 percent of the pairs did even one person report the crime ($p < .05$). Only three out of the 32 people who were tested in pairs told the receptionist that her money had been stolen.

If we consider only subjects who admitted noticing the theft, the results become even stronger. From the fact that 50 percent of Alone noticers reported, we would expect 75 percent of noticing pairs to include one reporter. Only 25 percent of these pairs did.

Subjects who noticed but did not report the theft often generated elaborate but somewhat implausible interpretations. "It looked like he was only making change," said several subjects. "I thought he took the money by accident," said one charitable soul. A number of subjects seemed to feel some conflict between their responsibilities to the receptionist and to law and order on the one hand and to the "obviously" poor (but well-dressed) college peer on the other. Some decided that not much money had been in the envelope after all. Each subject in the group condition, looking at the inactivity of the other bystander, seemed to be led to decide that the theft was not too serious and that squealing would be most inappropriate.

The results of this experiment, like those of the previous two, show that individuals may be less likely to take action in an emergency if others are present, even when the emergency involves a villain. Unlike the previous experiments, however, the effect was not sufficiently strong to overcome the fact that with two people present, there are twice as many people free to act. The theft was reported slightly, but not significantly, less often when two witnessed it than when one did. The receptionist was actually only slightly better off when one person saw her money stolen than when two did. This may indicate that the presence of a villain led to a smaller social inhibition effect than would occur in other situations. It may also indicate that, given the relatively low rate of response caused by the failure to notice the theft, there was little room for a larger effect to occur.

Experiment 9 provides a new test of social influence effects in a field setting and introduces a new variable, the number of villains.

EXPERIMENT 9. THE CASE OF THE STOLEN BEER

In Chapter 3, we pointed out several difficulties of laboratory experiments as contrasted to experiments carried out in the field. We pointed out that if the subject knows he is in an experiment, his experiences may have an "as if" quality about them, such that the subject feels he is only playacting. We suggested that many laboratory experiments subject people to strange situations and make strange requests of them. And we described some of the peculiar pressures on the subject, stemming in part from the fact that he is known by name to the experimenter.

In designing the laboratory experiments in this series, we tried to avoid these problems as much as possible. We staged our scenes in a waiting room where the subject sat before taking part in an interview. We used all the theatrical talent at our command to make the emergencies as realistic and plausible as possible (although, being emergencies, they were of necessity somewhat unusual). But, in each experiment, we knew the name of the subject (although, by policy, we forgot them as soon as the subject was finished). The relationships shown in these experiments would probably not have been different had they been conducted in field settings. To make sure, however, we designed an experiment to be conducted in the field, where subjects would be, and know they were, completely anonymous. Since the results of the theft experiment were somewhat complicated by the large number of people who claimed to have missed the action, we decided to repeat that experiment in a new setting. And we decided to add a new variable.

If the hypothesis that people will be importantly deterred from reporting a crime by the possibility of retribution from the villain is correct, then they should be more concerned the more vicious and the more numerous the villains are. In the last experiment, the Thief seemed a relatively mild-mannered, nonviolent young man. It is possible that he tended to generate feelings of sympathy at his poverty, rather than fear at his audacity and evil intent. It is possible that two Robbers would be a greater deterrent to intervention than one Thief. To test these possibilities, two Columbia undergraduates, Paul Bonnarigo and Malcolm Ross, turned to a life of crime.*

PROCEDURE

The Nu-Way Beverage Center in Suffern, New York, is a discount beer store. It sells beer and soda by the case, often to New Jerseyans who cross the state line to find both lowered prices and a lowered legal drinking age. During the spring of 1968 it was the scene of a minor crime wave—within one two-week period, it was robbed 96 times.

The robbers, husky young men dressed in T-shirts and chinos, followed much the same modus operandi on each occasion. Singly or in a pair, they would enter the store and ask the cashier at the check-out counter, "What is the most expensive imported beer that you carry?" The cashier, in cahoots with the Robbers, would reply, "Lowenbrau. I'll go back and check how much we have." Leaving the Robbers in the front of the store, the cashier would disappear into the rear to look for the Lowenbrau.

After waiting for a minute, the Robbers would pick up a case of beer near the front of the store, remark to nobody in particular, "They'll never miss this," walk out of the front door, put the beer in their car, and drive off. On 48 occasions, one Robber carried off the theft; on 48 occasions, two Robbers were present.

The robberies were always staged when there were either one or two people in the store, and the timing was arranged so that one or both customers would be at the check-out counter at the time when the Robbers entered. On 48 occasions, one customer was at the check-out

* This study is also reported in Latané, B. & Darley, J. M. Bystander "apathy." *American Scientist,* 1969, 57, 244–268.

counter during the theft; on 48 occasions, two customers were present. Although occasionally the two customers had come in together, more usually they were strangers. Sixty-one percent of the customers were male; 39 percent female. Since the check-out counter was about 20 feet from the front door, since the theft itself took less than one minute, and since the Robbers were both husky young men, nobody tried directly to prevent the theft. There were, however, other courses of intervention available.

When the cashier returned from the rear of the store, he came back to the check-out counter and resumed waiting on the customers there. After a minute, if nobody had spontaneously mentioned the theft, he casually inquired, "Hey, what happened to that man (those men) who was (were) in here? Did you see him (them) leave?" At this point, the customer(s) could either report the theft, say merely that he had seen the man or men leave, or disclaim any knowledge of the event whatsoever. Overall, 20 percent of the subjects reported the theft spontaneously, and 51 percent of the remainder reported it upon prompting. Since the results from each criterion followed an identical pattern, we shall report only the total proportion of subjects in each condition who reported the theft, whether spontaneously or not.

RESULTS

Fear of future retaliation from the Robbers did not seem to be a major concern of the bystanders. Doubling the number of Robbers made little difference in reporting the theft. Customers were actually somewhat, but not significantly, more likely to report the theft if there were two Robbers (69 percent) than if there was only one (52 percent, $p < .20$). This slight difference may be due to the fact that two Robbers were more visible and harder to ignore than one.

Sex of the bystander also had no effect on reporting; females were as likely to report as males.

As in each of our previous studies, the number of bystanders had an important effect on reporting the theft. Thirty-one of the 48 single customers, or 65 percent, reported the theft. From this, we would expect that 87 percent of the two-person groups would include at least one reporter. In fact, in only 56 percent of the two-person groups did even one person report the crime ($p < .01$). Social inhibition of reporting actually made the theft somewhat, though not significantly, less likely to be reported when two people saw it than when only one did.

DISCUSSION

In both the experiments reported in this chapter, subjects were more likely to report a crime if they alone witnessed it than if someone else saw it also. This effect, though strong, was not so strong as the comparable effects shown in previous chapters. The receptionist and the cashier were no better off if they had two people "minding the store" than if they had only one. In previous experiments, the social inhibition effect has been so strong that the emergencies have been less likely to be reported the more people who have been present.

For the first time in our studies, the agent that caused the emergency was a person. He may not have been a particularly admirable one, but even a bad man deserves some consideration. This divided the loyalties of our subjects. Regardless of what is abstractly right, reporting this emergency meant putting another person in trouble. It meant squealing. It meant balancing the rights of an individual against those of an institution. Many subjects may have chosen to side with the villain rather than with his victim. Even so, group size still proved a major determinant of bystander action.

9 MOTIVATION AND PERCEPTION IN EMERGENCIES

Although we have not gone into much detail on the subject, we have suggested that the reward-cost structure of an emergency situation may have important consequences for how a bystander will act. In this chapter, we would like to explore that reward-cost structure somewhat more fully and show that it may affect a bystander's perception as well as his actions.

The costs associated with emergencies can be high. A bystander faces costs whether or not he intervenes. If he does not intervene, he may feel empathic distress at a victim's continuing unhappiness, shame from the actual or implied reproach from other people, and guilt for failing to live up to his own standards of behavior. If he does intervene, he faces a wider array of possible costs.

Intervention will certainly cost time and effort; depending upon the circumstances, it may lead to other, less predictable costs. The intervening bystander may find himself confronted with the agent of disaster —the assailant may assault him, the fire may burn him. He may find himself subjected to ridicule or derision from other bystanders, who, themselves inactive, resent his example. He may find his actions misunderstood: stopping his car by the prostrate figure of a boy, he may have trouble convincing later arrivals that he was not the cause of the accident. The victim may spurn his help, attack him, later sue him, or even become completely dependent upon him. As if all this were not enough, social institutions often demand an accounting of emergencies. Even if the bystander's actions have been well-meaning and effective, he may find himself questioned and cross-examined by police, reporters, lawyers, prosecutors, and judges for months and years after the event. Perhaps worst of all, if he misinterprets the situation, he may find that for all of his efforts, he has only succeeded in making a fool of himself.

Costs for nonintervention tend to be psychological. They can be removed if the bystander can convince himself that there is no emergency. They are subject to distortion. They are subject to optimism: if the emergency resolves itself through no fault of the bystander, he need feel no guilt.

Costs for intervention tend to be material as well as psychological. They may involve immediate physical danger or discomfort or a more prolonged entrapment in legal tentacles. They may also involve fear or embarrassment. They are relatively unpredictable. The individual is thus left in the position of balancing the psychological discomforts of sympathy, fear of blame, and guilt against the unknown dangers of physical confrontation or legal involvement.

The rewards associated with emergencies generally are not high. Emergencies being what they are, nobody makes much profit from them. A nonintervening bystander certainly can expect no rewards. An intervening bystander can expect, at best, a newspaper write-up or a cash prize. These will accrue only if the emergency turns out to be really serious, his action "beyond the call of duty," and his intervention successful. Their likelihood is increased, but not much, if he suffers terribly as a result of his heroism. More generally, an intervener can expect nothing more than a hurried "Thanks."

This lack of rewards and prevalence of costs means that the bystander to an emergency is faced with a choice between two courses of action—both of them bad. If he fails to intervene, he may feel sympathy, shame, and guilt. If he attempts to intervene, he may suffer more material punishments. He risks making a fool of himself. The bystander presumably will not be especially happy with either of these choices. He is in an avoidance-avoidance conflict. How can he resolve it?

The easiest way out of such a conflict is for the bystander to convince himself that no emergency really exists. If he can keep from noticing the emergency (as many subjects were able to do in the theft study), if he can decide that the strange things he sees do not signify an emergency (as many subjects seemed to do in the smoke study), or if he can decide that the situation is not serious and that intervention would be inappropriate (as many subjects in the injured woman study decided), he need feel no conflict about whether or not to intervene. He need not worry about feeling guilty for sitting still or making a fool of himself for jumping up. He can relax.

The results of the experiments in Chapters 6, 7, and 8 indicate that people were powerfully influenced in their definitions of an emergency by the reactions of other people around them. Although the fact that people influence each other is old news to social psychologists, the strength of the influence was surprising. We suspect that one reason why social influence was so strong was that subjects *wanted* to believe that nothing really was wrong. If they could convince themselves from seeing the inaction of others that nothing was wrong, their conflict about action would be reduced. If they could decide that no emergency was happening, then the horns of their dilemma would turn out to be papièr mâché.

This line of thought suggests that there are pressures on the bystander to avoid noticing an emergency and to underestimate its seriousness. Are these pressures sufficient to affect his perception? Experiment 10, originally designed for another purpose, provides evidence relevant to this point. Experiment 10 was originally designed to explore the problems of introducing a minor variety of violence into an emergency, but after the first few subjects were run, it became obvious that the setting would not be useful for that purpose.

EXPERIMENT 10. "CHILDREN DON'T FIGHT LIKE THAT" *

Male Columbia undergraduates were recruited over the telephone to take part in a survey sponsored by the Consumer's Testing Bureau, a market research organization interested in testing the appeal of a number of adult games and puzzles. They were offered two dollars for their participation. Of 30 subjects contacted on the telephone, six had no time in which to make an appointment, and four did not arrive on time, leaving a total of 20 subjects in this experiment. All were freshmen and sophomores between the ages of 18 and 20.

When the subjects arrived for their appointments, they found themselves in front of two adjacent rooms. A sign on the door of one of the rooms read "Children's Testing Center," and on the other room, a sign read "Student's Testing Center." The two rooms were divided by a heavy collapsible curtain which was closed but unlocked. The student's

* We thank Judith Rodin for her help in conducting this study.

testing room was furnished with a table and chairs and a number of adult games were scattered about. A large sign giving preliminary instructions covered most of the one-way window in the room. None of the subjects realized that it was, in fact, a one-way glass.

Subjects were met at the door by the "market research representative," an attractive young woman, and shown to the testing room. The young woman explained the purpose of the survey and asked the subjects to fill out a preliminary questionnaire containing items dealing with the subject's background and game-playing preferences. Before leaving the subject with his questionnaire, the interviewer mentioned that she was going out for coffee and would return in 15 minutes to complete the session. She also remarked, "By the way, you will notice that next door there are two children from a nearby elementary school who are playing by themselves now. They will be tested later by another branch of the Consumer Testing Bureau interested in children's games. I notice that they do tend to get a little noisy, but I hope they won't bother you." During this time sounds of two children playing with toys filtered through the collapsible curtain. The experimenter then left the room and the subject began to work on his questionnaire.

The emergency. The sounds of the two children continued after the interviewer left the room. After six or seven minutes of relatively quiet play, one of the children, older by voice and manner than the other, asked the younger to "Give me that toy." The younger child refused, and the older asked again. Again the younger child refused. The older child threatened, "If you don't give me that toy, I will beat you up." Still the younger child refused. When the older began to hit him, however, he gave in, saying, "Take the toy, you can have it!" But the older shouted, "It's too late. You didn't give it to me when I asked for it. Now I'm going to really beat you up." The fight increased in violence and intensity over a four-minute period as the bully began seriously to hurt the victim, who yelled, "I give up, stop it. You can have it. Get off me. You cut me. It hurts so much. Help me, please, I'm bleeding." But the bully didn't stop. "I'm going to beat you up," he shouted. "You asked for it, I'm going to really beat you up." Finally, after several more minutes of violence, an adult male entered the room, admonished the children for fighting, and took them off.

This whole sequence, of course, was prerecorded on a stereophonic tape and played over a high fidelity sound system in the next room. The children who made the tape, although not professional actors, had apparently had sufficient experience at squabbling to give what sounded to us like a very convincing performance.* During the fight, the collapsible curtains shook and rattled, and loud thumps were produced in the next room.

RESULTS

Our major interest, of course, was how long it would take the subject, hearing a bully beating up a younger child in the next room, to come to the assistance of the victim. Of 12 subjects run in this condition, however, only one took any action whatever. He left the room by the door and reported the fight to the first person he saw. The other 11 subjects sat in the room and continued to work on their questionnaires throughout the entire course of the fight and for a minute afterward until the interviewer returned to the room to begin the postexperimental interview.

Before concluding too quickly that Columbia students are heartless or cruel, or do not feel it necessary to protect the safety of grade-school children, it should be noted that the major reason for their inaction was a simple one. They did not believe in the reality of the fight. Of the 12 subjects in this condition, nine developed alternative interpretations, while only three accepted the fight as real.

According to their postexperimental reports, none of the subjects suspected that they were listening to a tape until the fight actually began. Throughout the entire seven-minute play sequence, they believerd that there were children next door. Once the fight began, however, subjects began to change their interpretation. Their explanations varied: several subjects thought there were children next door listening to a radio or watching a TV fight. Others convinced themselves that the sequence sounded like a tape recording, but did not interpret this as having any bearing upon themselves. Only one subject suspected that the tape was being used to test his reactions.

Several subjects admitted that they were unsure what really was happening, but that they were sure that it wasn't a fight. "Children don't fight like that," they said. "It went on too long." Or, "Once he gave back the toy, the other one should have stopped beating him up. If it had been a real kid, he would have." These subjects were right; children don't usually fight like that. But then, most other emergencies are rather unusual too.

All subjects assured the interviewer that had the fight been real,

* We thank Ross Koppenaal and his friend Alan for their performance.

they would have been among the first to intervene. Although their statements sound rather smug, we do not doubt their sincerity. Subjects in this experiment, as in the previous ones, seemed no more apathetic, no more indifferent to the suffering of others or to feelings of social responsibility than the rest of this generation of college students. They seemed genuinely convinced that there was no fight in the next room.

Since the interpretation that the sounds of the fight came from a tape recording was actually correct, the simplest explanation for this result is that the tape was poorly made and unconvincing. A second explanation, based upon the fact that subjects decided that they were hearing a tape only when the fight faced them with the responsibility for action, is that subjects were motivated to disbelieve the reality of the situation by their desires to avoid involvement. Having made the tape, we preferred this explanation, and, after the first few disbelieving subjects convinced us that the situation was not suitable for our original purposes, decided to change the experiment to test this explanation. After the first three of the above subjects had been run, we added a new condition to this experiment in which we expected there to be fewer pressures to disbelieve in the fight.

No responsibility condition. If subjects in the above condition were motivated to avoid believing in the reality of the fight by their desire to avoid conflict over whether or not to intervene, we would expect that subjects who were exposed to the same situation *minus* the responsibility to themselves take action might be more likely to believe in the fight. In order to test this, a second condition was run in this experiment. This new condition duplicated the first with but one exception. Instead of saying, "There are children who are playing by themselves," the interviewer told the subject that "Somebody is in there testing them now. I have noticed that they do tend to get a little noisy, but please leave them alone." The tape was then played as before. The two conditions were exactly comparable with the exception that in the second condition, since somebody was already in the room with the children, the subject himself was not responsible.

The results provide strong support for the perceptual distortion hypothesis. Of eight subjects run in this No Responsibility condition, all but one fully believed that two children were in the next room and having a fight. Only one subject thought it was a tape. This proportion is significantly different from that found in the initial Responsibility condition ($p < .02$).

TABLE 11
Frequency of Believing the Fight Was Real

Condition	N	Believe	Not Believe
Responsibility (Children are alone)	12	25%	75%
No responsibility (Children are supervised)	8	88%	12%

Subjects in the No Responsibility condition were no more likely to try to break up the fight than Responsibility subjects: only one of the eight attempted to intervene, and he did so by opening the curtain and going into the next room. But they did believe in the fight. They got upset at the supervisor who was in the room with the children and they could not understand why he was so lax as to let one child beat up another, but they did believe in the fight.

The different results in the two conditions cannot be attributed to differential attention to the fight. Subjects in the No Responsibility condition were as likely to mention the fight spontaneously during the postexperimental interview as were subjects in the Responsibility condition, and were as able to quote things the subjects had said. The difference can probably best be explained by the fact that subjects in the Responsibility condition seemed actively to try to convince themselves that they were hearing a tape. Seven of the nine who disbelieved the fight said that they had thought about going in, and then had decided it was a tape, as if to alleviate all responsibility and misgiving by assuring themselves that the fight was not real.

DISCUSSION

The results of this experiment suggest that individuals, through a process of rationalization, may inhibit their own response to an emergency in which they feel conflict about intervening by distorting their perceptions of the situation so as to believe that no emergency is in fact occurring. They can thus remain guiltlessly aloof.

10 SOCIAL DETERMINANTS OF BYSTANDER INTERVENTION II: DIFFUSION OF RESPONSIBILITY

So far, we have devoted our attention entirely to the first two stages of our model of the intervention process: noticing the event and deciding it is an emergency. Before moving on, let us review the theory to date and assess the support it has received.

NOTICING THE EVENT

We suggested that individuals might be less likely to notice an emergency when they are in the presence of others, since, in public, it is embarrassing to be too attentive to others. This suggestion received only partial support. Subjects in the smoke-filling room were slower to notice the smoke when there were others present, but this effect was rather small, significant only statistically. Subjects were not slower or less likely to notice the theft of money when others were present. All subjects in the injured woman study seemed to notice her accident immediately, and it was impossible to determine how quickly subjects noticed the beer robbery.

The relationship between the proprieties of public behavior and attentiveness to emergencies is probably more complex than we suggested. To take a far-fetched example, a shy person on a factory tour may listen intently to the guide to avoid embarrassing eye contacts with strangers. If the gesticulating guide backs into a machine, the shy person will be the first to notice; he may never notice a straggler slumping to the floor with a heart attack. Proper public behavior often, but by no means always, makes a person less likely to notice an emergency.

DECIDING IT IS AN EMERGENCY

Once a person notices an event, he must interpret it. The chances are that his interpretation will be shaped by the presence of other people. Other people should inhibit the actions and reactions of each individual so that, as each looks around to see what others are doing, he will see only nonresponsive bystanders and be led to remain inactive himself. Consequently, individuals should be less likely to intervene in an emergency when they are in public than when they are alone.

This prediction received strong support in each of the experiments in which it was tested. The basic results are shown in Table 12. In each of these experiments, individuals were significantly less likely to

TABLE 12
Percentages of Single Subjects or Groups Helping

Experiment:	Alone (N)	Expected Together	Obtained Together (N)
Experiment 6. Smoke	75 (24)	98	38 (8 trios)
Experiment 7. Injured Woman	70 (26)	91	40 (20 pairs)
Experiment 8. Money Theft	23 (25)	41	19 (16 pairs)
Experiment 9. Beer Robbery	65 (48)	87	56 (48 pairs)

perform a socially responsible act if they were in the presence of others than if alone. In the first two, this effect was so strong that the emergency was significantly less likely to be dealt with, the more people who were available to help.

The overall results gave good support to the theory; so did our interviews with subjects after the experiments. Subjects who did not intervene explained their inaction in terms of their interpretations of the situations. They did not act because they thought there was no emergency, or that the emergency was not serious, or that it would be inappropriate to act. They seemed convinced by their explanations; even though the children's fight showed that perceptions were affected by the subjects' motivations as well as by the presence of other people, we think that subjects were sincere in their beliefs. We think they were correct when they stated that if their interpretations had been different, they would have intervened.

Surprisingly, in each of these experiments, subjects were unaware of, or unwilling to admit to, the fact that they had been influenced by the other people present. In the injured woman study where subjects were least inhibited by friends and most by the passive confederate, subjects thought they had been most influenced by friends and least by the passive confederate.

Social influence, then, turns out to be a major determinant of bystander intervention in emergencies—even though bystanders may not be aware that they are being influenced. Similar social influence processes, we believe, can account for many of the cases of bystander "apathy" appearing in the newspapers. They can account for incidents such as the Andrew Mormille murder, in which 11 subway passengers rode with a dying boy through several stops before anyone reported the stabbing. They can account for incidents where crowds of passersby have gathered to watch an emergency, but have remained passive in the face of need.

Need we go further? Cannot these social influence processes explain all failures to intervene? No. One more step in the decision model is required: once an individual has noticed an event and interpreted it as being serious, he still has to decide what, if anything, he personally will do about it. He must decide that he has a responsibility to help and that there is some form of assistance that he is in a position to give. He is faced with the choice of whether he himself will intervene. Even at this stage, the presence of other people can affect his action.

DECIDING ON PERSONAL RESPONSIBILITY

Let us look again, with Rosenthal, at the Genovese case:

> Catherine Genovese, known as Kitty, returned in death to cry the city awake. Even then it was not her life or her dying that froze the city, but the witnessing of her murder—the choking fact that thirty-eight of her neighbors had seen her stabbed or heard her cries, and that not one of them, during that hideous half-hour, had lifted the telephone in the safety of his own apartment to call the police and try to save her life.

"In the safety of his own apartment." Alone. Each observer was literally walled off from the others. Seeing shadowy shapes backlit against other windows, each observer knew that others also watched but he could not tell what they were doing. Unable to judge their reactions, he could not be influenced by them. Knowing that the others were unable to see what he did, he was not inhibited by their presence. Obviously, the explanations we have developed so far do not fit this case. Yet no one called the police.

Although each individual could not see the actions of others and knew that they could not see his, still each individual was aware that other bystanders were also witnessing the murder. Knowing this, each bystander may have felt a diffusion of his personal responsibility for taking action. The responsibility for helping was diffused among the bystanders, and, being diffused, was diminished.

THE DIFFUSION OF RESPONSIBILITY

If only one bystander is present at an emergency, he carries all of the responsibility for dealing with it; he will feel all of the guilt for not acting; he will bear all of the blame that accrues for nonintervention. If others are present, the onus of responsibility is diffused, and the finger of blame points less directly at any one person. The individual may be more likely to resolve his conflict between intervening and non-intervening in favor of the latter alternative.

When only one bystander is present at an emergency, if help is to come it must be from him. Although he may choose to ignore them (out of concern for his personal safety or desire "not to get involved"), any pressures to intervene focus uniquely on him. When there are several observers present, however, the pressures to intervene do not focus on anyone; instead, the responsibility for intervention is shared among all the onlookers. As a result, each may be less likely to help.

Potential blame may also be diffused. However much we wish to think that an individual's moral behavior is divorced from considerations of personal punishment or reward, there is both theory and evidence to the contrary. It is perfectly reasonable to assume that, under circumstances of group responsibility for a punishable act, the punishment or blame that accrues to any one individual is often slight or non-existent.

Finally, if others are known to be present but their behavior cannot be closely observed, any one bystander may assume that one of the other observers is already taking action to end the emergency. If so, his own intervention would only be redundant—perhaps harmfully or confusingly so. Thus, given the presence of other onlookers whose behavior cannot be observed, any given bystander can rationalize his own inaction by convincing himself that "somebody else must be doing something."

It is possible to look at all of these factors as reductions in the psychological costs of nonintervention. Whether or not they are conceptualized this way, however, they do suggest that even when bystanders to an emergency cannot see or be influenced by each other, the more bystanders who are present, the less likely any one bystander will be to intervene and provide aid. To test this, it would be necessary to create an emergency situation in which each subject is blocked from communicating with others to prevent his getting information about their behavior during the emergency. The experiment reported in the next chapter attempted to fulfill this requirement.

11 AN EPILEPTIC SEIZURE

Even if a person has noticed an event and defined it as an emergency, the fact that he knows that other bystanders also witness it may still make him less likely to intervene. The others may inhibit intervention because they make a person think that *his* responsibility is diffused and diluted. Each soldier in a firing squad feels less personally responsible for killing a man as a member of a group than he would if he alone pulled the trigger. Likewise, any individual in a crowd of onlookers may feel less responsibility for saving a life than if he alone witnessed the emergency.

If your car breaks down on a busy highway, hundreds of drivers whiz by without anyone's stopping to help; if you are stuck on a nearly deserted country road, whoever passes you first is apt to slow down and stop. The extent of personal responsibility that a passerby feels makes the difference. An individual driver on a lonely road knows that if he does not stop to help, the person will not get help; the same individual on the crowded highway will feel he personally is no more responsible than any of 100 other drivers. So even though an event clearly is an emergency, any individual in a group who sees an emergency may feel less responsible simply because any other bystander is equally responsible for helping.

To test this line of thought, an emergency was simulated in a setting designed to resemble Kitty Genovese's murder. Subjects overheard a victim calling for help. Some knew that they were the only one to hear the victim's cries; others believed that other people besides themselves were aware of the victim's distress. As with the Genovese witnesses, subjects could not see each other or know what the others were doing, so the kind of direct group inhibition found in the smoke, injured woman, and theft studies could not operate.

EXPERIMENT 11. A FIT TO BE TRIED *

A college student arrived in the laboratory and was ushered into an individual room from which a communication system would enable him to talk to the other participants. It was explained to him that he was to take part in a discussion about personal problems associated with college life and that the discussion would be held over the intercom system, rather than face-to-face, in order to avoid embarrassment by preserving the anonymity of the subjects. During the course of the discussion, one of the other subjects underwent what appeared to be a very serious nervous seizure similar to epilepsy. During the fit it was impossible for the subject to talk to the other discussants or to find out what, if anything, they were doing about the emergency. The dependent variable was the speed with which the subjects reported the emergency to the experimenter. The major independent variable was the number of people the subject thought to be in the discussion group.

PROCEDURE

Male and female students in introductory psychology courses at New York University were contacted to take part in an unspecified experiment as part of a class requirement. Upon arriving for the experiment, the subject found himself in a long corridor with doors opening off it to several small rooms. An experimental assistant met him, took him to one of the rooms, and seated him at a table. After filling out a background information form, the subject was given a pair of headphones with an attached microphone and was told to listen for instructions.

Over the intercom, the experimenter explained that he was interested in learning about the kinds of personal problems faced by normal college students in a high-pressure, urban environment. He said that to avoid possible embarrassment about discussing personal problems with strangers several precautions had been taken. First, subjects would remain anonymous, which was why they had been placed in individual

* Portions of this study are reported in Darley, J. M. & Latané, B. Bystander intervention in emergencies: Diffusion of responsibility. *Journal of Personality and Social Psychology*, 1968, 8, 377–383. We thank Susan Darley for her help.

rooms rather than face-to-face. (The actual reason for this was to allow tape recorder simulation of the other subjects and the emergency.) Second, since the discussion might be inhibited by the presence of outside listeners, the experimenter would not listen to the initial discussion, but would get the subject's reactions later, by questionnaire. (The real purpose of this was to remove the obviously responsible experimenter from the scene of the emergency.)

The subjects were told that since the experimenter was not present, it was necessary to impose some organization. Each person would talk in turn, presenting his problems to the group. Next, each person in turn would comment on what the others had said, and finally, there would be a free discussion. A mechanical switching device would regulate this discussion sequence and each subject's microphone would be on for about 2 minutes. While any microphone was on, all other microphones would be off. Only one subject, therefore, could be heard over the network at any given time. The subjects were thus led to realize when they later heard the seizure that only the victim's microphone was on and that there was no way of determining what any of the other witnesses were doing, nor of discussing the event and its possible solution with the others. When these instructions had been given, the discussion began.

In the discussion, the future victim spoke first, saying that he found it difficult to get adjusted to New York City and to his studies. Very hesitantly, and with obvious embarrassment, he mentioned that he was prone to seizures, particularly when studying hard or taking exams. The other people, including the real subject, took their turns and discussed similar problems (minus, of course, the proneness to seizures). The naive subject talked last in the series, after the last prerecorded voice was played.*

The emergency. When it was again the victim's turn to talk, he made a few relatively calm comments, and then, growing increasingly loud and incoherent, he continued:

I-er-um-I think I-I need-er-if-if could-er-er-somebody er- er-er-er-er-er-er- give me a little-er-give me a little help here because-er-I-er-I'm-er-er- h-h-having a-a-a real problem-er-right now and I-er-if somebody could

* To test whether the order in which the subjects spoke in the first discussion round significantly affected the subjects' speed of report, the order in which the subjects spoke was varied (in the six-person group). This had no significant or noticeable effect on the speed of the subjects' reports.

help me out it would-it would-er-er s-s-sure be-sure be good . . . be-cause-er-there-er-er-a cause I-er-I-uh-I've got a-a one of the-er-sei------er-er-things coming on and-and-and I could really-er-use some help so if somebody would-er-give me a little h-help-uh-er-er-er-er c-could somebody-er-er-help-er-uh-uh-uh (choking sounds). . . . I'm gonna die-er-er-I'm . . . gonna die-er-help-er-er-seizure-er (chokes, then quiet).*

The experimenter began timing the speed of the real subject's response at the beginning of the victim's speech. Informed judges listening to the tape have estimated that the victim's increasingly louder and more disconnected ramblings clearly represented a breakdown about 70 seconds after the signal for the victim's second speech. The victim's speech was abruptly cut off 125 seconds after this signal, which could be interpreted by the subject as indicating that the time allotted for that speaker had elapsed and the switching circuits had switched away from him. Times reported in the results are measured from the start of the fit.

Group size variable. The major independent variable of the study was the number of other people that the subject believed also heard the fit. By the assistant's comments before the experiment, and also by the number of voices heard to speak in the first round of the group discussion, the subject was led to believe that the discussion group was one of three sizes: either a two-person group (consisting of a person who would later have a fit and the real subject), a three-person group (consisting of the victim, the real subject, and one confederate voice), or a six-person group (consisting of the victim, the real subject, and four confederate voices). All the confederates' voices were tape-recorded.

Time to help. The major dependent variable was the time elapsed from the start of the victim's fit until the subject left his experimental cubicle. When the subject left his room, he saw the experimental assistant seated at the end of the hall, and invariably went to the assistant. If 6 minutes elapsed without the subject having emerged from his room, the experiment was terminated.

As soon as the subject reported the emergency, or after 6 minutes had elapsed, the experimental assistant disclosed the true nature of the experiment, and dealt with any emotions aroused in the subject. Finally, the subject filled out a questionnaire concerning his thoughts

* We thank Richard Nisbett for his magnificent performance as the victim.

and feelings during the emergency, and completed a number of personality scales, to be discussed in the next chapter.

RESULTS

Plausibility of manipulation. Judging by the subjects' nervousness when they reported the fit to the experimenter, by their surprise when they discovered that the fit was simulated, and by comments they made during the fit (when they thought their microphones were off), one can conclude that almost all of the subjects perceived the fit as real. There were two exceptions in different experimental conditions, and the data for these subjects were dropped from the analysis. Both of these subjects had recently been in an experiment on conformity, at the end of which they had been carefully told that "the voices you have heard over the intercom were not real; they were tape-recorded as part of the experiment."

Effect of group size on helping. The number of bystanders that the subject perceived to be present had a major effect on the likelihood with which he would report the emergency (Table 13). Eighty-five percent of the subjects who thought they alone knew of the victim's plight reported the seizure before the victim was cut off, while only 31 percent of those who thought four other bystanders were present did so ($p < .02$).

Every one of the subjects in the two-person groups, but only 62 percent of the subjects in the six-person groups, ever reported the emergency. The cumulative distributions of response times for groups of

TABLE 13
Effects of Group Size on Likelihood and Speed of Response

Group size	N	Percent responding by end of fit	Percent ever responding	Time in seconds
2 (Subject and victim)	13	85	100	52
3 (Subject, victim, and one other)	26	62	85	93
6 (Subject, victim, and 4 others)	13	31	62	166

different perceived size (Figure 4) indicates that, by any point in time, more subjects from the two-person groups had responded than from the three-person groups, and more from the three-person groups than from the six-person groups.

Ninety-five percent of all the subjects who ever responded did so within the first half of the time available to them. No subject who had not reported within 3 minutes after the fit ever did so. The shape of these distributions suggests that had the experiment been allowed to run for a considerably longer time, few additional subjects would have responded.

Speed of response. To achieve a more detailed analysis of the results, each subject's time score was transformed into a "speed" score by taking the reciprocal of the response time in seconds and multiplying by 100. The effect of this transformation was to deemphasize differ-

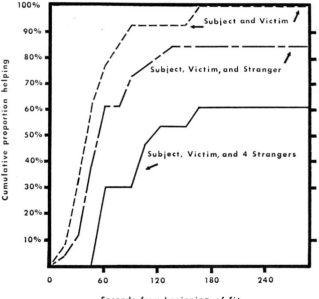

FIGURE 4
Cumulative proportion of subjects reporting seizure who think they alone hear the victim, or that one of four others also are present

ences between longer time scores, thus reducing the contribution to the results of the arbitrary 6-minute limit on scores. A high speed score indicates a fast response.

An analysis of variance indicates that the effect of group size is highly significant ($p < .01$). Duncan multiple-range tests indicate that all but the two- and three-person groups differ significantly from one another ($p < .05$).

Victim's likelihood of being helped. An individual subject is less likely to respond if he thinks that others are present. But what of the victim? Is the inhibition of the response of each individual strong enough to counteract the fact that with five onlookers there are five times as many people available to help? From the data of this experiment, it is possible mathematically to create hypothetical groups with one, two, or five observers.* The calculations indicate that the victim is about equally likely to get help from one bystander as from two. The victim is considerably more likely to get help from one or two observers than from five during the first minute of the fit. For instance, by 45 seconds after the start of the fit, the victim's chances of having been helped by the single bystanders were about 50 percent, compared to none in the five-observer condition. After the first minute, the likelihood of getting help from at least one person is high in all three conditions.

Reasons for intervention or nonintervention. After the debriefing at the end of the experiment each subject was given a 15-item checklist and asked to check those thoughts which had "crossed your mind when you heard Subject 1 calling for help." Whatever the condition, each subject checked very few thoughts, and there were no significant differences in number or kind of thoughts in the different experimental groups. The only thoughts checked by more than a few subjects were: "I didn't know what to do" (28 percent), "I thought it must be some sort of fake" (31 percent), and "I didn't know exactly what was happening" (40 percent).

It is possible that subjects were ashamed to report socially undesirable rationalizations, or, since the subjects checked the list *after* the true nature of the experiment had been explained to them, their memories might have been blurred. It is our impression, however, that most

---

* The formula for the probability that at least one person will help by a given time is $1 - (1 - P)^n$ where n is the number of observers and P is the probability of a single individual (who thinks he is one of n observers) helping by that time.

subjects checked few reasons because they had few coherent thoughts during the fit.

We asked all subjects whether the presence or absence of other bystanders had entered their minds during the time that they were hearing the fit. Subjects in the three- and six-person groups reported that they were aware that other people were present, but they felt that this made no difference in their own behavior.

DISCUSSION

Subjects, whether or not they intervened, believed the fit to be genuine and serious. "My God, he's having a fit," many subjects said to themselves (and were overheard via their microphones) at the onset of the fit. Others gasped or simply said "Oh." Several of the male subjects swore. One subject said to herself, "It's just my kind of luck—something has to happen to me!" Several subjects spoke aloud of their confusion about what course of action to take: "Oh God, what should I do?"

When those subjects who intervened stepped out of their rooms, they found the experimental assistant down the hall. With some uncertainty, but without panic, they reported the situation. "Hey, I think Number 1 is very sick. He's having a fit or something." After ostensibly checking on the situation, the experimenter returned to report that "everything is under control." The subjects accepted these assurances with obvious relief.

Subjects who failed to report the emergency showed few signs of the apathy and indifference thought to characterize unresponsive bystanders. When the experimenter entered her room to terminate the situation, the subject often asked if the victim was "all right." "Is he being taken care of?" "He's all right isn't he?" Many of these subjects showed physical signs of nervousness: they often had trembling hands and sweating palms. If anything, they seemed more emotionally aroused than did the subjects who reported the emergency.

Why, then, didn't they respond? It is our impression that nonintervening subjects had not decided *not* to respond. Rather, they were still in a state of indecision and conflict concerning whether to respond or not. The emotional behavior of these nonresponding subjects was a sign of their continuing conflict, a conflict that other subjects resolved by responding.

The fit created a conflict situation of the avoidance-avoidance type.

On the one hand, subjects worried about the guilt and shame they would feel if they did not help the person in distress. On the other hand, they were concerned not to make fools of themselves by overreacting, not to ruin the ongoing experiment by leaving their intercoms, and not to destroy the anonymous nature of the situation, which the experimenter had earlier stressed as important. For subjects in the two-person condition, the obvious distress of the victim and his need for help were so important that their conflict was easily resolved. For the subjects who knew there were other bystanders present, the cost of not helping was reduced and the conflict they were in more acute. Caught between the two negative alternatives of letting the victim continue to suffer or the costs of rushing in to help, the nonresponding bystanders vacillated rather than chose not to respond. This distinction may be academic for the victim, since he got no help in either case, but is an extremely important one for arriving at an understanding of the causes of bystanders' failures to help.

Although the subjects experienced stress and conflict during the experiment, their general reactions to it were highly positive. On a questionnaire administered after the experimenter had discussed the nature and purpose of the experiment, every single subject found the experiment either "interesting" or "very interesting" and was willing to participate in similar experiments in the future. All subjects felt they understood what the experiment was about and indicated that they thought the deceptions were necessary and justified. All but one felt they were better informed about the nature of psychological research in general.

In this study, no subject was able to tell how the other subjects reacted to the fit. (Indeed, there were no other subjects actually present.) The effects of group size on speed of helping, therefore, were due simply to the perceived presence of others rather than to the influence of their actions. This means that the experimental situation was unlike emergencies such as a fire, in which bystanders interact with each other. It was similar to emergencies such as the Genovese murder, in which spectators knew others were also watching, but were prevented from communication that might have counteracted the diffusion of responsibility. Experiments in previous chapters, however, have shown that the kinds of communication (for the most part, nonverbal) that seem to occur in emergencies are not likely to counteract diffusion.

Variations in composition of the bystander group. Encouraged by the correlation between the size of the group and the speed with which the individual reported the seizure, we went on to make other variations in the experimental situation. If varying the *number* of people witnessing an emergency affects the degree of responsibility felt by any one, it is possible that varying the *kind* of people might also. For example, one might feel less responsible for dealing with certain emergencies if a policeman were present. Since we could not see any plausible way of introducing a policeman into the seizure situation, we decided instead to vary the sex of the several observers heard to be present.

In our culture, it seems to be the male's duty and prerogative to respond to emergencies. It is the female's duty to watch and admire the male. There are certain exceptions to this, of course, but most emergencies, particularly those in which there is any danger to the respondent, are the responsibility of the male. In particular, we thought, restraining a thrashing male with a seizure should be seen as a man's job.

To test this hypothesis, we varied the sex of the real subject and that of the other observer in the three-person group. We chose the three-person group because we felt that, since there was only one other observer present, any variation in his characteristics would have the most impact on the subject.

In one condition, the real subject (who was a female) thought that the other bystander was a female. In a second condition, she thought that the other witness was a male, and in the third, male college sophomores were the experimental subjects, and the other observer was a female. Since coping with emergencies is a male duty, we expected that the female subjects would be less likely to report the emergency when the other bystander was a male than when the other was a female. Also, we expected that male subjects would react more quickly than female subjects.

Table 14 shows that none of these expectations was confirmed. Not only are the differences not significant; they are not even marginally significant. Nor, to use the last resort of the writer with no results, "are the differences in the direction suggested by the hypothesis." It is obvious from the table that there are no important differences in speed of individual reaction caused by the variations of composition of the three-person group.

To push this rather surprising finding to the limit, we did one other variation in composition of the three-person group. In this condition the subject was a female, and she heard the other observer

TABLE 14

Effects of Group Composition on Likelihood and Speed of Response *

Group Composition	N	Percent responding by end of fit	Time in seconds
Female S, male other	13	62	94
Female S, female other ·	13	62	92
Female S, male medic other	5	100	60
Male S, female other	13	69	110

* Three-person group, male victim.

identify himself as a premedical student who worked in the emergency ward at Bellevue Hospital. Since the other observer was both a male and a premedical student, experienced in dealing with emergencies, it was expected that the female subjects would certainly leave coping with the emergency to him. As Table 14 indicates, not even this prediction was confirmed.

Males helped no faster than females, and females were not slowed in their helping when the other bystander was a male, or even a medically-trained male. How can this lack of results be explained? In the clear light of hindsight, it is obvious that our predictions were based on normative considerations. A male should react more quickly to the emergency than a female. Why? Because it is what is expected of him. That is, because it is *normative*. Considering what we have said elsewhere about the remote relationship that prevails between norms and actual behavior of specific situations, it was inconsistent of us to expect this particular experimental variation to have any effect.

By this graceful confession of lack of forethought, we might have charmed you into considering the ineffectiveness of variations of group composition as supporting our position on the nonpredictive nature of norms. We must point out, however, that the result can be explained in another way. Previously, we distinguished between two classes of interventions. "Direct" intervention, such as stepping in and breaking up a fight, putting out a fire, or swimming out to save a drowning person, often requires skill, knowledge, and physical strength. It may well involve danger. It may be that cultural norms dictate male responsibility

only for this. "Reportorial" intervention involves reporting the emer
gency to somebody who is qualified to handle it. Calling the police or
sounding the fire alarm are examples of this rather low-cost kind of
intervention. Because it is low-cost there is no clear norm requiring male
action. Anyone, male or female, can call for help.

In the seizure study, subjects clearly saw the required intervention
as being reportorial in nature. Both postexperimental interview data and
subjects' verbal reports to the experimenter indicated that the subject
intended to report the emergency to the experimenter rather than go
directly to the aid of the victim, whose exact location they did not
know. Therefore, male-female norms, although relevant to high-cost
direct intervention, were not applicable to the low-cost reportorial inter
vention needed in this experiment.

Although this line of argument seems plausible, we are not entirely
convinced by it. It may be that sex is simply not a very important de
terminant of how people react to emergencies. In general, in our studies
we have found no differences due to sex. Females were no less and no
more likely than males to correct the (sometimes vicious) misinforme
in the subway experiment reported in Chapter 3. Females were no less
likely than males to report the beer robbery in Chapter 8. And in the
present experiment, females were no less likely to act. The only differ
ence we have found between the response of males and females to a
request for help occurred in Experiment 2, in which students asked
for twenty cents for the subway. Males were more likely to give than
females, but that might be entirely due to the fact that it is easier for
a male to reach into his coat pocket than for a female to open her pocket
book, rummage through it until she finds her change purse, and then
rummage through the pennies until she finds two dimes.

Variations in acquaintanceship. In contrast to the strong effect pro
duced by the group size manipulation, no variation in group composition
had thus far produced any changes in speed of reporting the emergency
We did however try one more variation in composition of the group
This time, when we contacted the subject by telephone to schedule
her for the experiment, we asked her to bring a friend (most subject
who could arrange to have a friend available at the various possible
times were willing to bring one). Again, we ran the three-person con
dition, but this time we modified our experimental apparatus and the
instructions to accommodate two real bystanders, the subject and the
friend that she brought with her. Otherwise, the experiment was ex

ctly as before. Again the victim had the fit, and again, we timed the peed with which the subjects reacted to it.

Many people, in discussing the failure of bystanders to intervene n an emergency, comment that this would never happen in small towns, vhere everybody is acquainted with everybody else. It is possible that hey are right. In Experiment 7, where the experimenter fell off a chair, pairs of friends responded more quickly than did pairs of strangers. since increasing the *number* of people present at an emergency has the ame effect on responding whether or not subjects can see each other, ve were curious as to whether friendship would also.

RESULTS

Fourteen pairs of friends, or 28 subjects, were run in this condition. Their performance is shown in Table 15. Subjects who thought their riends were present were more likely to report the emergency, and lid so faster ($p < .01$) than were subjects who thought a stranger was here. (It should be noted that in this experiment, unlike those in vhich groups were in each other's physical presence, it was appropriate o use the average response for each person, and not just the fastest person in a pair.) Friends were significantly faster than strangers; in

TABLE 15
Effects of Friendship with Other Subject on Likelihood and Speed of Response

Condition	N	Percent responding by end of fit	Percent ever responding	Time in seconds
Subject, victim, and stranger	26	62	85	93
Subject, victim, and friend	28	75	100	58
Subject and victim	13	85	100	52

act, their average speed is not significantly slower than that of subjects n the two-person groups, who believed themselves to be alone with the victim.

Figure 5 presents the cumulative proportion of subjects responding over the course of the experiment. At every point in time, more sub-jects who thought their friends were present had reported the emergency than subjects who thought a stranger was present. Even though subjects could not communicate with their friends and could not see what they were doing, they still reported the emergency faster. Why?

Two lines of explanation suggest themselves. First, of course, un-like the other experimental conditions, the subject knows that she will meet her friend after the experiment and almost certainly will discuss the emergency with her. Realizing this when the emergency occurs, the subject may react quickly in order to maintain her friend's good opinion.

This explanation suggests that although responsibility is diffused, there is a counterforce increasing the speed of report, and the two cancel each other out. An alternative explanation is also possible. With two acquaintances present, the responsibility may not be diffused at all.

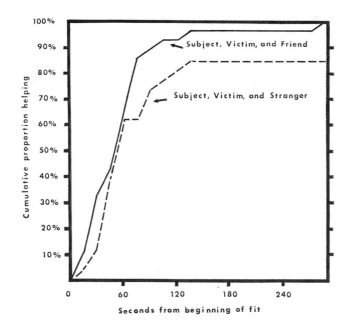

FIGURE 5

Cumulative proportion of subjects reporting seizure who think a stranger or a friend also hears the victim

Instead of a situation where there is "me" and a stranger, there is simply "we," and "we" have 100 percent of the responsibility. Responsibility may not diffuse across friends.

In discussions after the experiment, subjects could give us no information that would help discriminate between these two explanations. In fact, they claimed adamantly that they had not been influenced by knowing their friends were present. As in previous experiments, subjects were strongly influenced, but seemed unaware that this influence had taken place.

Some interesting things did come out in the postexperimental discussion. First, there was no tendency for the "host"—the person who brought the other girl with her to the experiment—to report faster. Second, although we asked a variety of questions to get at which partner in the friendship was the leader or dominant partner, no answer predicted which of the subjects in the pair reported fastest. Finally, the length of time over which the pair had been friends, which ranged from ten minutes in the case of one resourceful subject who captured a stranger as her partner on the way to the experiment, to ten years in the case of another subject who had known her partner since grade school, did not correlate with the speed with which the fastest of the partners reported the emergency or with the average of the two partners' time to report.

We had thought that subjects who had been acquainted a long time might have developed a division of responsibility or leadership, so that it clearly would be the task of one of the partners to cope with the emergency while the other one stayed out of the way. This was not the case. Although the presence of a friend as the other bystander increased the subject's response speed in comparison with the other three-person conditions, the subjects behaved independently of each other when they emerged from their rooms to report the emergency.

Acquaintance with the victim. In this experimental setting, it is possible to vary one more kind of acquaintance—whether the subject had previously had any contact with the victim. Even a slight degree of acquaintanceship might make a major difference in the speed of response. Anything that would take away the feeling that the victim was a faceless stranger, we suspected, might greatly increase his chances of getting help. Accordingly, we arranged for subjects in still another condition to have a brief and apparently accidental encounter with the victim before the experiment.

By the time we were ready to run this variation, the student who had made the original tape recording of the seizure had graduated and gone on to teach at another university. Since we despaired of finding anyone else of his exceptional skills (as an actor, not an epileptic) to make a new tape, we searched around for somebody with a voice that could pass for his. Luckily, we found a student with almost the same voice quality and accent, a student who could pass for an undergraduate and who was willing to lurk in the hall before our experiment and pass for one of the subjects. He was stationed in the hall to which the subject had to come for the experiment and was trained to strike up a casual conversation with the subject when she appeared. They talked about topics having nothing to do with the experiment.

Less than a minute after the conversation began, the experimenter appeared and led the two into their separate cubicles, saying as he did so that the confederate would be the first subject (to insure the subject's realizing that this was indeed the person who later had the fit). Then the regular tape for the six-person condition was played, the victim had his fit, and we timed the speed with which the subject reacted. The six-person condition was used to give maximum scope for any possible increase in response speed.

RESULTS

As Table 16 shows, merely meeting the victim-to-be briefly had a major effect on the likelihood and the speed with which subjects went to his assistance ($p < .05$). The effect was so strong that subjects who met the victim were not significantly slower than subjects in the two-person groups to report the emergency. Figure 6 shows that at every point in time, more subjects who had met the victim had intervened than had unacquainted subjects. Overall, they took an average of less than half the time to do so.

One explanation for this strong effect might suggest that the subject assumed that he was the only person to have met the victim. If so, he might feel that the responsibility for helping the victim devolved especially on him. He was somehow closer to the victim than any of the other subjects and could not diffuse his responsibility onto them so easily. It would be interesting to see if the same increased help would occur in a two-person situation, where this explanation would not apply. We suspect it would.

TABLE 16

Effect of Acquaintance with the Victim on Likelihood
and Speed of Response

Condition	N	Percent responding by end of fit	Percent ever responding	Time in seconds
Subject, victim, and 4 strangers (Subject did not meet victim)	13	31	62	166
Subject, victim, and 4 strangers (Subject met victim)	12	75	100	69
Subject and victim (Subject did not meet victim)	13	85	100	52

A second explanation emerged from the postexperimental interviews with the subjects. Subjects in this condition, and *only* in this condition, reported that when the victim began to have the fit, they could visualize him doing so. They could *picture* an actual individual in distress. It may be that this ability to visualize the victim so increased the amount of empathy or sympathy that subjects felt for him that they were quicker to respond to his need.

A final explanation would suggest that just as the subject had had a chance to see the victim, he knew that the victim had had a chance to see him. He may have felt more accountable to the victim, in much the same way that friends in the last variation may have felt more accountable to each other. In sharp contrast to the strong emphasis on anonymity that prevailed in the rest of the experiment, the victim has seen the subject and might recognize him if they later ran into each other on the campus. This could be a particularly painful meeting if the subject had failed to help the victim in distress.

DISCUSSION

We have suggested two distinct processes which might lead people to be less likely to intervene in an emergency if there are other people

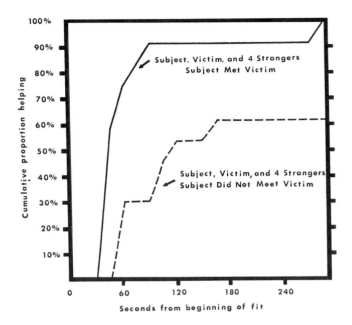

FIGURE 6
Cumulative proportion of subjects in six-person condition who had or had not met victim reporting the seizure

present than if they are alone. First, we have suggested that the presence of other people may affect the interpretations each bystander puts on the ambiguous signals of an emergency situation. If other people are present at an emergency, each bystander will be guided by the public manifestations of their private reactions in formulating his own impressions. Unfortunately, the visible public reactions of others may not be a good indication of their true feelings and judgments. It is possible for a state of pluralistic ignorance to develop, in which each bystander is led by the *apparent* lack of concern of the others to interpret the situation as being less serious than he would if alone. To the extent that he does not feel the situation is an emergency, of course, he will be unlikely to take any helping action, an effect which was demonstrated in the smoke, injured woman, and beer robbery studies.

Even if an individual does decide that an emergency is actually in process and that something ought to be done, he still is faced with the choice of whether he himself will intervene. Here again, the presence of other people may influence him—largely by reducing the costs associated with nonintervention. If a number of people witness the same event, the responsibility for action is diffused and each may feel less necessity to help, a result which was demonstrated in the seizure experiment.

Need both these decision steps be included in the intervention model? Might not either the social influence or the diffusion of responsibility decision account for all the data? We think not. For example, the diffusion explanation cannot account for the significant difference in response rate between the strangers and confederates conditions in the injured woman experiment. There should be equal diffusion in either case. This difference can more plausibly be attributed to the fact that strangers typically did not show such complete indifference to the accident as did the stooge. The diffusion process also does not seem applicable to the results of the smoke experiment. Responsibility for protecting oneself from fire should not diffuse. On the other hand, social influence processes cannot account for results in the seizure experiment. Subjects in that experiment could not communicate with each other and thus could not be influenced by each other's reactions.

Although both processes probably operate, they may not do so at the same time. To the extent that social influence leads an individual to define the situation as nonserious and not requiring action, his responsibility is eliminated, making diffusion unnecessary. Only if social influence is unavailable or unsuccessful in leading subjects to misinterpret a situation should diffusion play a role.

Indirect evidence supporting this analysis comes from observation of nonintervening subjects in the various emergency settings. In settings involving face-to-face contact, as in the smoke and injured woman experiments, noninterveners typically redefined the situation and did not see it as a serious emergency. Consequently, they avoided the moral choice of whether or not to take action. During the postexperimental interviews, subjects in these experiments seemed relaxed and assured. They felt they had behaved reasonably and properly. They were not anxious.

In the seizure experiment, on the other hand, face-to-face contact was prevented, social influence could not help subjects define the situation as nonserious, and they were faced with the moral dilemma of whether or not to intervene. Although the imagined presence of other people led many subjects to delay intervention, their conflict was exhibited in the postexperimental interviews, in which, it will be remembered, subjects who did not intervene seemed more emotionally aroused than did subjects who reported the emergency—further evidence for the existence of two separate and distinct processes.

12 PERSONALITY, SOCIOECONOMIC CLASS, AND HELPING IN EMERGENCIES

We have asked why people sometimes help and sometimes fail to help others in distress and have described a number of situational variables which markedly influence the response to emergencies. Another question may also be relevant. Why do some people help and other people fail to help others in distress? Do people differ in their willingness to intervene in emergencies?

Many common explanations for bystander "apathy" would assert that they do. A careful reading of numerous off-the-cuff explanations suggests that many commentators believe that *motivational* problems lie at the root of failures to intervene. Some suggest that people no longer care about the fate of others, they are apathetic, they are indifferent, they no longer have human feelings about other human beings. Others claim that unresponsive bystanders are alienated. They no longer believe in the principles underlying our society, they see no reason to follow its rules, they do not care what others think of them.

If bystander inaction can be explained by such enduring personality traits as apathy or alienation, then we would expect that people who most possess those traits would be least likely to take action. Although we claimed in Chapter 3 that such general motivational forces as compassion (the opposite of apathy) or adherence to social norms (the opposite of alienation) are not very good answers to the question of why people will act in some but not other situations, they may be more adequate in explaining why some, but not other, people act.

PERSONALITY CORRELATES OF HELPING BEHAVIOR

Psychologists have devised a wide variety of paper-and-pencil personality tests, many of which have shown impressive correlations with each
other and with actual behavior. Out of the diversity of well-validated
and potentially relevant scales, we were able to choose only a few, since
we felt there was a limit to our subjects' patience. Consequently, we
tried to pick scales which would most probably relate to helping.

Subjects who participated in the seizure study were asked, after
they had finished the experiment, to fill out several personality scales.
All agreed to do so. They filled out the Social Responsibility Scale designed by Berkowitz and Daniels, a measure of the extent to which
subjects accept the social responsibility norm. They filled out the Mar-
lowe-Crowne Need for Approval Scale, a measure of the extent to
which subjects try to present a desirable image of themselves by claim-
ing to behave supernormatively. And they filled out a battery of scales
designed by Richard Christie. Included in this battery are his versions
of the authoritarian personality scale (the F Scale), a scale of anomia,
or alienation from social norms and institutions, and his Mach Scale.
The last test measures subjects' tendencies to agree with the writings
of Machiavelli, a man we would hardly expect to go out of his way to
save anybody except a prince. All of these scales have shown impressive
validity—they relate in important ways to the manner in which people
behave.

None of these personality variables predicted helping. Their failure
is shown in Table 17. Their lack of correlation cannot be attributed to
low sample size, since N's ranged from 60 up, which would have made
a correlation of .25 statistically significant. This sample size was obtained by normalizing the scores within each experimental condition and
then pooling the scores across all conditions. Even after this, not one
of the five personality variables correlated significantly with helping.
The most potent of these scales accounted for only a minor amount of
variance, 4 percent, beyond that attributable to experimental conditions.

Obviously, it cannot be concluded from this that an individual's
personality does not affect his helping in emergencies. Only a much
more limited conclusion is possible: the variables cited, as they were
measured, did not predict reporting the seizure. Still, to us and to other
psychologists whom we asked for advice, these scales seemed quite rele-

TABLE 17
Personality Correlates of Standardized Speed of Reporting the Seizure

Personality test	r
F scale (Christie's revision)	+.20
Anomia (Christie's revision)	−.10
Christie's Machiavellianism Scale	+.08
Marlowe-Crowne Need for Approval Scale	+.04
Berkowitz Social Responsibility Scale	−.02

Note: The correlation coefficient r, indicates the degree of relationship between two variables, with .00 indicating no relationship and 1.00 indicating a perfect relationship.

vant to predicting who would and who would not help. In general, we found our failure to demonstrate personality correlates of helping somewhat discouraging, although, of course, further research may well uncover other variables which are more effective, or other situations in which more effects occur.

There are, however, reasons why personality should be rather unimportant in determining people's reactions to the emergency. For one thing, the situational forces affecting a person's decision are so strong that the individual faced with an emergency does not have time to think; he must make a quick decision under strong pressure. It is possible, under such circumstances, that personality variables do not have much room for play. Christie, for example, has found that his Mach Scale predicts behavior only when the individual is given "latitude for improvization." If his responses are constricted by the situation, a high Mach cannot outmaneuver a low.

A second reason why personality differences may not lead to differences in overt behavior in an emergency is that they may operate in opposing ways at different stages of the intervention process. For example, a tender-hearted person who really wants to help may be too frightened or squeamish to do so. The person who can take a cold-eyed look at an emergency and see it as dangerous may be cold-hearted when it comes to acting. McGuire has suggested an analogous reason for the inconsistent and often nonexistent relationships between personality and attitude change. Fearfulness, stupidity, or low self-esteem, he suggests, may all make a person more likely to yield to a persuasive message, but less likely to comprehend it in the first place, balancing out the amount of change shown by subjects varying in these traits.

Although we can only offer these very tentative explanations for the failure of personality variables to correlate with helping behavior, that failure does create serious difficulties for one class of commonly given explanations for the failure of bystanders to intervene in actual emergencies: those explanations involving apathy, alienation, or indifference. These explanations generally assert that people who fail to intervene are somehow different from the rest of us, that they are "alienated by industrialization," "dehumanized by urbanization," "depersonalized by living in the cold society," or "psychopaths."

These explanations serve a dual purpose for those who adopt them. First, they answer (if only in a superficial way) the puzzling and frightening question of why people watch others die without trying to save them. Second, they give individuals reason to deny that they too might fail to help in a similar situation.

The results of this experiment seem to indicate that such personality variables may not be as important as these explanations suggest. Alienation, Machiavellianism, acceptance of social responsibility, need for approval, and authoritarianism did not predict the speed or likelihood of help. In sharp contrast, the perceived number of bystanders did. The explanation of bystander "apathy" may lie more in the bystander's response to other observers than in presumed personality deficiencies of "apathetic" individuals. Although this realization may force us to face the guilt-provoking possibility that we too might fail to intervene, it also suggests that individuals are not, of necessity noninterveners because of their personalities. If people understand the situational forces that can make them hesitate to intervene, they may better overcome them.

BIOGRAPHICAL CORRELATES OF HELPING BEHAVIOR

Subjects in the seizure situation also filled out a set of autobiographical items. This was rather a mixed collection of items, chosen with one eye towards reasonable correlates of helping behavior, but with the other eye firmly fixed on the possibilities of serendipity (indeed, we included questions on birth order, that reflex choice of any social psychologist concerned with serendipity). Other items included father's education, the subject's age, year in college, church attendance, and so on. In general, these items tended to correlate somewhat more highly with helping behavior than did the personality variables (with the exception of birth order), but still, only two reached an acceptable level of significance.

These items concerned the size of the community in which the subject grew up and the occupation of the subject's father. The smaller the size of the community in which the subject grew up, the more likely she was to help the victim of the emergency (r = .26, p < .05). This correlation is not particularly strong, but it must be remembered that "the size of the community in which I grew up" is somewhat restricted, for our subjects almost invariably came from towns in and around New York. Given this restriction of range, we were somewhat surprised to find any correlation at all. This finding may provide some comfort for those small town residents who claim "It couldn't happen here."

Father's social class, as coded from his occupation, related −.24 (p = .06) with helping. Again, choosing subjects from a college population can be expected to truncate the range of the variable, but the finding does indicate that there is a slight tendency for lower middle-class people to be faster to help than upper middle-class people. This seems an interesting variable, and so we followed it into another study.

TABLE 18
Biographical Correlates of Standardized Speed of Reporting the Seizure

Item	r
Size of community in which S grew up	−.26
Father's occupation	−.24
Length of stay in NYC	−.18
Number of siblings	+.18
Church attendance	−.17
Age	+.14
Father's education	−.12
Number of generations in USA	−.08
Year in college	−.05
Lived with parents during childhood	+.04
Birth order	.00

SOCIAL CLASS, ENVIRONMENTAL FAMILIARITY, AND EMERGENCY FUNCTIONING

Socioeconomic class, of course, is not a psychological variable. The problem for psychologists is to specify which variables, among those mediated by social class, determine a person's helping behavior. To test the effect of one variable that might mediate between socioeconomic class and helping behavior, the following field experiment was conducted.

EXPERIMENT 12. SUBWAYS ARE SAFER THAN AIRPORTS

A clean-cut young man on crutches, his left knee bent and heavily taped, laboriously made his way toward his plane or train. Unfortunately, as he approached a single male sitting far enough away from other people to be functionally isolated, the young man tripped and fell to the ground, clutching his knee in great pain. A confederate, stationed some distance away, unobtrusively observed the incident and noted the by-stander's reactions.

Sixty such incidents were staged in each of two public locations, an underground subway station and La Guardia Airport. The results were startlingly different. In the subway 83 percent of the people helped; in the airport only 41 percent did ($p < .01$). This result obviously implies a socioeconomic difference. Middle- and upper-class citizens, who are much more likely to be present at airports, seem less inclined to help others. They may put a higher value on the privacy of others and thus be less likely to intrude even when the others are in distress. Lower classes, who are more frequently found in subways, have no such inhibitions.

Roger Granet, who ran the studies as a class project at New York University, had a rather different hypothesis in mind. His expectation was that familiarity with the environment was the determining factor. The major reason for greater helpfulness in subways is that subway users grow familiar with the subway setting in a way that few people ever do with airports.

To determine whether familiarity influenced functioning in emergency situations, after each bystander had responded to the staged incident, another experimenter appeared to interview him about his familiarity with subways or airports. Subjects were asked about how often they used the facility and their knowledge of its entrances, exits, telephone booths, etc. The questionnaire was short and the person administering it, though good-natured, was large. There were very few refusals to answer. One other variable was also coded: the socioeconomic class of the subject, as judged from the external cues of dress and bearing.

As we would expect, the socioeconomic class of bystanders in the airport was higher than that of bystanders in the subway. People were, on the average, considerably less familiar with the airport environments. More subtle results also conformed to our general expectations: the higher the socioeconomic class of the respondent the *more* likely he was to be familiar with the airport and the *less* likely he was to be familiar with the subway station. These correlations mainly served to give us some confidence in the validity of the environmental familiarity questionnaire and the observer's rating of the socioeconomic class of the subject.

The correlations of these variables with the subjects' helping responses emerged quite clearly. In both the airport ($r = .29$) and the subway ($r. = .31$) there was a significant ($p < .05$) correlation between familiarity and responding to the emergency. In neither case was there a significant correlation between social class and helping behavior. As one would expect from this pattern of results, the relationship between familiarity and emergency functioning was not much affected by partialing out the effect of socioeconomic class. The overall pattern of the results was clear: increased familiarity with a setting is associated with an increase in the helping behavior. Socioeconomic class is not.

Granet's interpretations of these results seems to us to be the appropriate one: a person who is more familiar with the environment is more aware of the way in which the environment works. He is not overloaded with stimuli and his fears of embarrassment or, in the subway, actual physical harm, have moderated. He may have a greater stake in keeping that environment safe. He is "in control." Thus he is more likely to help. Clearly, environmental familiarity is one variable that may often mediate the relationship between socioeconomic class and emergency functioning. Another such mediating variable might be past experience with emergencies: lower class people may simply have seen more emergencies, and be less disoriented by them when they occur.

DISCUSSION

As we have seen, individual difference variables account for remarkably little variance in helping behavior. None of the personality tests we have investigated have related to helping, and autobiographical informa-tion seems to do little better. These findings suggest that anybody can be led either to help or not to help in a specific situation. Characteristics of the immediate situation may have a more important influence on what the bystander does than his personality or life history. These findings further suggest that motivational deficiencies may not account for the unresponsive bystander. The question with which we opened this chapter, "Why do some people help and other people fail to help others in distress?" may have been a false lead.

13 MAN'S STRENGTH TO COMFORT MAN'S DISTRESS

In Chapter 4 we presented a theoretical model of the intervention process. We suggested that before a bystander will intervene in an emergency, he must *notice* that something is happening, *interpret* that event as an emergency, and decide that he has *personal responsibility* for coping with it. If a person fails to take any of these steps in a direction favoring intervention, he will fail to intervene. In Chapter 5, we hypothesized that the presence of other people may make the bystander less likely to take each of these steps.

In general, the results of our studies have provided good evidence supporting this line of thought. Subjects in groups have been somewhat, but not always, slower to notice an emergency than single subjects. Subject in groups have been less likely than single subjects to interpret a potential emergency as serious or intervention as the proper course of action. And even when they know an emergency is occurring, subjects who think others are present have been less likely to take personal responsibility than subjects who think they alone know of the victim's distress. The results of our studies, however, have also led us to modify some of our ideas about the intervention process.

MODIFICATIONS OF THE DECISION MODEL

Cycling. Originally, we thought a person faced with a potential emergency would take each decision in sequence. A person must notice an

121

event before he worries about its definition. He must also define the event as an emergency before he worries about whether he is responsible for intervening. The trouble with this view is that the bystander is not committed to his decisions until and unless he finally steps forward to help. Instead, he can cycle back and forth. For instance: "The smoke coming out of that isolated building means it's on fire." "My God, I ought to run in and try to save anybody who's inside." "That seems like an awful risk—I wonder if it is really on fire."

The results of the children's fight support this new picture. They suggest that motivations appropriate to later stages in the decision process affect earlier decisions.

Blocking. We expected that subjects would proceed through the decision tree and decide whether or not to help. In general, that is what they did—with one important exception. Subjects in the seizure experiment who were unable to convince themselves that the victim's cries for help did not represent an emergency did not necessarily come to a decision. Many subjects responded. The ones who did not did not seem to have decided *not* to respond; rather, they made no decision at all and remained transfixed at the decision point. In some cases at least, the unresponsive bystander may be confused and conflicted, rather than alienated and depersonalized.

Commitment. Although a subject may honestly be undecided, the longer he waits in indecision, the harder it is for him subsequently to intervene. A person who reacts immediately on seeing smoke trickling into a room has an obvious reason for his reaction. A person who jumps up and leaves the room four minutes after the smoke has begun might feel that he is behaving inconsistently. By sitting through the first four minutes, he has committed himself to an interpretation of the situation which is inconsistent with his later leaving. The commitment may be public—he would look foolish—but it also may be private. As Bem and others have suggested, an individual is capable of observing himself to determine what he must be thinking.

Subjects in our experiments responded early or not at all. Over 90 percent of all subjects who responded responded within the first half of the relatively short time available to them. In each of the experiments in which time was a variable, we had the strong impression that even had we let the emergencies continue forever, few additional subjects would have acted. By their initial indecision and inaction, subjects inadvertently committed themselves to continued inaction.

GENERALITY OF FINDINGS

The results of these experiments suggest that social inhibition of bystander intervention may be rather general over a wide variety of emergency situations. The research we have reported has utilized emergencies involving danger to the subject and danger to a victim. Some emergencies involved a villain and others did not. Some were quite serious, involving even life and death, while others were only moderately serious. In each of these situations, bystanders were less likely to intervene if other bystanders were also present.

The experiments utilized a wide variety of subject populations, including male and female members of the general public as well as college students of both sexes. Studies were conducted both in the laboratory and in the field. All of these subject populations and both of these settings produced the social inhibition effect.

There was some hint, minor to be sure, that subjects from large cities were less likely to intervene quickly than subjects from the suburbs or from smaller towns. It may be that city dwellers are in general less likely to help than townspeople. It may also be that social inhibition effects are less strong for townspeople than for urbanites. Further research should answer these questions. We see no reason to expect a different *pattern* of results from nonurban subjects, although the *intensity* of effect might be less strong.

In one important sense, the results of these experiments should not be generalized too far. It is tempting, for example, to conclude that people are more likely to report smoke (70 percent) than they are to report the theft of money (23 percent) even when they are alone. Such a conclusion would be totally unjustified. The base rates of intervention in the various experimental emergencies reflect a multitude of factors peculiar to the way each one happened to be set up in the laboratory. It would certainly be possible to alter the smoke setting in such a way as to lower the rate of response drastically, merely by varying such arbitrary things as the size of the room, the density of smoke, the fire-resistance of the building material, the ease of exit, etc. The absolute rates of response in each experiment mean little by themselves.

They do acquire meaning, however, when we compare conditions within experiments. In this case, all the arbitrary features of the experimental setting were constant across conditions and cannot be used to account for differences in response between conditions. The absolute rate of response cannot be generalized to other possible emergencies; the relationship between conditions can.

AWARENESS OF SOCIAL INFLUENCE

During each of the postexperimental interviews, we asked our subjects whether they thought they had been influenced by the presence of other people. We asked this question every way we knew how: subtly, directly, tactfully, bluntly. Always we got the same answer. Subjects persistently claimed that their behavior was not influenced by the other people present. This denial occurred in the face of results showing that the presence of others did inhibit helping.

Conformity, in our society, is a rather unpopular trait, and it may have been that subjects were not about to admit that they had conformed, especially when conformity meant failing to help in an emergency. However, for what it is worth, our impression is that this motivation was relatively unimportant in leading subjects to deny social influence. People seem quite sincerely and genuinely unaware of the various ways in which they are influenced in their definitions of physical and social realities by the behavior of other people.

To test the generality of this finding, we carried out paper-and-pencil replications of the smoke and seizure experiments. We described each situation objectively and carefully and asked subjects what they would do. For half the subjects, the situations were described as if they alone were present at the scene of the emergency; half the subjects were told they were with other people, either two other people waiting for an interview (smoke replication) or as part of a six-person discussion group (seizure replication). All subjects rated themselves as highly likely to help, and equally likely to help whether they were alone or together. Next, we asked the Alone subjects to imagine that other people had been present and the Together subjects to imagine that they were alone. Nobody thought it would make any difference. In general, subjects rated themselves as extremely likely to react, regardless of the circumstances.

We thought this might be a social desirability effect, so we changed the nature of the questions and asked subjects to imagine not themselves but an average college student in the same situations. The typical subject thought that the average college student would be a little less likely to react helpfully than he himself would be, but they did not expect that the presence or absence of other observers would make him more or less likely to help.

The results of our actual experiments, then, seem counterintuitive. This has various technical advantages, largely concerning demand characteristics. It demonstrates the importance of doing actual experiments—armchair speculation or "as if" role playing would lead to different and wrong conclusions. This fact also has substantive implications: people systematically underestimate the degree to which they are influenced by other people. Moderate conformers to a man, we think of ourselves as sturdy independents. A study of the tactics people use to deny they are victims of social influence ought to be interesting and rewarding.

FURTHER RESEARCH

We have by no means exhausted research on this subject. Although we would not like to make the trite claim that we have raised more questions than we have answered, there are a number of obvious directions in which we feel further research could be profitably taken. For example, although we have some confidence that the inhibiting effects of other people are due to several distinct processes, it would be useful to delimit these more precisely and to weigh their relative contributions.

We have suggested four different reasons why people, once having noticed an emergency, are less likely to go to the aid of the victim when others are present: (1) Others serve as an audience to one's actions, inhibiting him from doing foolish things. (2) Others serve as guides to behavior, and if they are inactive, they will lead the observer to be inactive also. (3) The interactive effect of these two processes will be much greater than either alone; if each bystander sees other bystanders momentarily frozen by audience inhibition, each may be misled into thinking the situation must not be serious. (4) The presence of other people dilutes the responsibility felt by any single bystander, making him feel that it is less necessary for himself to act.

Each of these explanations involves different channels of communication among bystanders. The diffusion of responsibility explanation requires only that a bystander believe others to be present; he does not have to see them or they him. The audience inhibition hypothesis requires that the other bystanders see him but not that he see them.

The social influence explanation requires that he see the others, but not that they see him. Finally, the interactive process requires full visual communication. It should be possible to isolate these various effects by systematically varying the channels of communication open to bystanders within a single emergency setting.

A second line for further research emerges from the consistent finding that the inhibiting effects of other bystanders are lower if they are friends, and that a bystander is more likely to go to the assistance of a victim if he has had prior personal contact with him. Two types of explanation can be given for these results. On the one hand, they may be due to the fact that the subject *knows* the other bystander (and is less likely to be misled by his inaction or less likely to want to shove responsiblity onto him) or knows the victim (and feels more compassion for him). On the other hand, they may come about because the subject *is known by* the victim or the other bystanders and thus feels more accountable. It would be interesting to investigate the importance of these factors by setting up one-way contacts, that is, situations where the subject knows the victim but is not known by him, and vice-versa.

Another line of research might investigate the question of whether the unresponsive bystander lives only in our large cities. Although we have suggested that the findings of our studies point out a number of situational variables that might make a victim less likely to get help in a city than in a town, there is still some indication that city dwellers might be generally less responsive than townspeople.

> Do the work that's nearest,
> Though it's dull at whiles,
> Helping, when we meet them,
> Lame dogs over stiles.

In the century since it was written, this minor bit of exhortatory doggerel has become sheer camp. Urban Americans have become too sophisticated to appreciate the style. Many think Americans have also become too cynical to appreciate the moral and too alienated to follow it. The results of our studies suggest not that people are too alienated to "help lame dogs," but that they are, instead, overly responsive to a variety of social pressures which inhibit the urge to help others. Susceptibility to social influence rather than alienation from social values may be the major deterrent to altruism. Too much concern for other bystanders rather than too little for the victim may be the key to the unresponsive bystander.

The results of our experiments show that situational variables such as the number of other people present are more important determinants of intervention in emergencies than apathy or alienation. They suggest that the "threefold cord" of Ecclesiastes may not be broken, but only stretched a little by the conditions of modern urban life. They suggest reasons why the failure to intervene may be characteristic of our modern cities.

When an emergency occurs in a large city, many people are likely to be present. The people are likely to be strangers. It is likely that no one will be acquainted with the victim. The bystanders may be unfamiliar with the locale of the emergency. These are exactly the conditions that made helping least likely in our experiments.

"There's safety in numbers" according to an old adage, and modern city dwellers seem to believe it. They shun deserted streets, empty subway cars, and lonely walks in dark parks, preferring instead to go where others are or stay at home. When faced with stress, both animals and men seem less afraid when they are in the presence of others. When faced with stress, both men and animals seek the company of others.

It may be that people are less likely to find themselves in trouble if there are others present. But if a person does find himself in trouble, safety in numbers may be illusory. While it is certainly true that a victim is unlikely to receive help if nobody knows of his plight, our research casts doubt on the suggestion that he will be more likely to receive help if more people are present. In fact, the opposite seems to be true. A victim may be more likely to get help or an emergency to be reported, the fewer people who are available to take action.

Although the results of these studies may shake our faith in safety in numbers, they also may help us begin to understand a number of frightening incidents where crowds have listened to but not answered a call for help. Newspapers have tagged these incidents with the label "apathy." We have become indifferent, they say, callous to the fate of suffering others. Our society has become "dehumanized" as it has become urbanized. These glib phrases may contain some truth, since startling cases such as the Genovese murder often seem to occur in our large cities, but such terms may also be misleading. Our studies suggest a different conclusion. They suggest that situational factors, specifically factors involving the immediate social environment, may be of greater importance in determining an individual's reaction to an emergency than such broad motivational concepts as "apathy" or "alienation due to urbanization." They suggest that the failure to intervene may be better understood by knowing the relationship among bystanders rather than that between a bystander and the victim.

In a less sophisticated era, Rudyard Kipling prayed "That we, with Thee, may walk uncowed by fear or favor of the crowd; that, under Thee, we may possess man's strength to comfort man's distress." The conjunction of these two apparently unrelated hopes proves astute; it appears that the latter hope may depend to a surprising extent upon the former.

REFERENCES

Allen, H. Unpublished doctoral dissertation, New York University, 1968.

Berkun, M. M., Bialek, H. M., Kern, R. P., and Yagi, K. Experimental studies of psychological stress in man. *Psychological Monographs,* 1962, **76,** 1–39 (Whole No. 534).

Darley, J. M. Fear and social comparison as determinants of conformity behavior. *Journal of Personality and Social Psychology,* 1966, 4, 73–78.

Darley, J. M., and Latané, B. Bystander intervention in emergencies: Diffusion of responsibility. *Journal of Personality and Social Psychology,* 1968, **8,** 377–383.

Foy, E., and Harlow, A. F. *Clowning Through Life.* E. P. Dutton & Co., 1928.

Latané, B. Field studies of altruistic compliance, *Representative Research in Social Psychology,* 1970, **1,** 49–61.

Latané, B., and Darley, J. M. Bystander "apathy." *American Scientist,* 1969, **57,** 244–268.

Latané, B., and Darley, J. M. Group inhibition of bystander intervention. *Journal of Personality and Social Psychology,* 1968, **10,** 215–221.

Latané, B., and Rodin, Judith. A lady in distress: inhibiting effects of friends and strangers on bystander intervention. *Journal of Experimental Social Psychology,* 1969, **5,** 189–202.

Rosenthal, A. M. *Thirty-Eight Witnesses.* McGraw-Hill, 1964.

INDEX